REVIVIFY

REVIVIFY

RESTORING FAILED LEADERS

JASON MITCHEM

WestBow
PRESS
A DIVISION OF THOMAS NELSON

WestBow Press books may be ordered through booksellers or by contacting:

WestBow Press
A Division of Thomas Nelson
1663 Liberty Drive
Bloomington, IN 47403
www.westbowpress.com
1-(866) 928-1240

Because of the dynamic nature of the Internet, any Web addresses or links contained in this book may have changed since publication and may no longer be valid. The views expressed in this work are solely those of the author and do not necessarily reflect the views of the publisher, and the publisher hereby disclaims any responsibility for them.

ISBN: 978-1-4497-0400-1 (sc)
ISBN: 978-1-4497-0401-8 (dj)
ISBN: 978-1-4497-0462-9 (ebk)

Library of Congress Control Number: 2010933997

Printed in the United States of America

WestBow Press rev. date: 07/21/2011

Acknowledgments

I want to thank my loving wife, April, for all the encouragement and support she gave me during the process of my restoration and writing of this project. The ability to love me through the hardest times has been an inspiration to me beyond description. I love you. To my two wonderful children, Devin and Jaysa; you are some of the most talented young people I know and I thank God that he chose me to be your dad. Thank you for loving me even when I blew it so badly. I love you both.

I would be remiss not mention one of the greatest pastors, teachers, uncles, and dads I know. Uncle Wesley, thank you for taking a chance on me. You taught me that restoration can come even to a failed leader such as me. You have truly shown me what a servant of Christ looks like and that it is possible to love unconditionally. Hey, just one more time.

To my father-in-law, Pastor Randy Blizzard, who has always believed in me when others did not. From my first job in Las Vegas, through my business failures and successes, you have been a constant source of faith and belief. Thank you for teaching me how to believe in myself and believe even more in a God who has your back. Thank you for showing me how to bounce back. I love you.

To my friend and confidante Rodney Baker, your friendship and support have been a sustaining force in my life. You propped me up when I had no strength to stand. You cleaned me up when I was a mess. You listened to me vent my frustrations and hurts when no one else would. You have been a faithful friend beyond description. This book would not have been possible without your generous financial contribution. I will always love you, my friend. Friends forever and together in his service.

I also want to acknowledge some of the greatest people I know: Herbe and Jana Smith. What does one say about friends that have been there through thick and thin and yet love you all the way through? Words would not do justice to express the beauty of you both. I love you and will endeavor to live a life worthy of your friendship and love.

Dedication

I want to dedicate this book to Pastor Wesley McClain. If it were not for you, this book would not be possible. Thank you for being my inspiration, counselor, pastor, and "just one more time" partner. I love you.

re·viv·i·fy —*verb (used with object),* to restore to life; give new life to; revive; reanimate.

Micah 7:8 (NLT)
Do not gloat over me, my enemies!
For though I fall, I will rise again.
Though I sit in darkness,
the Lord will be my light.

Contents

For the Failed Leader

Final Thoughts

Introduction

It has been experienced in every place of worship on the face of the planet. It has been experienced in just about every organization, and without doubt, it has been seen in the halls of our government. I am talking about leaders who fail. From the White House to God's house, and even your house failed leaders have made their human natures known.

As long as mankind has been in existence, failed leaders have taken their place on the pages of history. The first leader to fail was Adam. He was only responsible for himself and Eve and yet he failed to keep it together. When leaders succumb to their human natures, it creates a firestorm of emotions for those within their sphere of influence. Because of this pain, the natural reaction is to take them out and remove them from their positions of honor forever. I have to ask you why. Why do we so adamantly seek their punishment and removal without the chance of return? For those who dare try, they are considered men and women of poor values and compromise.

There is a confusing quote out there that says, if at first you don't succeed, try, try again." However, for whatever reason, this does not seem to apply to leaders who fail and let their followers down. But maybe that is just it. They have followers. Where did we get the idea that leaders are supposed to have followers? Now, by natural course of events, anyone who leads the charge, whether it is in a place of business or a church, will ultimately have people that follow their lead. However, somewhere in the process we that follow their lead forget that they, too, are as human as the next person. So when they fail, it completely takes us by surprise. For whatever reason, we put leaders at the top of the food chain and require them not to be human any longer.

As of the writing of this book, two very prominent Republican leaders announced that they, too, were human and admitted to moral failure: Senator John Ensign of Nevada and Governor Mark Sanford of South Carolina, both of whom have been mouthpieces for the conservative movement and cried for accountability and integrity. Yet, when they made their startling announcements, people all over this country called for their complete and immediate resignation from office. Once again, it came as a shock to their followers. The question is whether leaders should be held accountable to a higher standard than the average person. Some are quick to say yes. I, too, believe that they should. But to say that their failure permanently disqualifies them from positions of leadership is judgmental and hypocritical at best.

How many average-joe parents out there have committed some of the same mistakes these leaders have admitted to? Yet, does this disqualify them as parents? Does this say they are not good dads and good moms? Hardly! And no one calls for them to give up their children and never parent or be a participating member of a family again. So what do we do with them? If you are a pastor, you work with them and restore them in hopes of bringing them back to a place of honorable leadership within their respective homes and families. If you are business leader, you work with the offending member of that organization and do what you can to make them productive again. In both cases, you help them to capitalize on the failure itself to teach them and create in them strength and understanding. You restore them. If at first you don't succeed, try, try again.

I also want to add that by no means am I trying to say that what is written in the pages of this book is the authority on the matter of restoring failed leaders. It is my intent and desire to start a worldwide dialogue. I want religious organizations to reconsider their bullheaded stances, and businesses to join the effort of rescuing talented leaders that would otherwise be thrown away.

Within the chapters of this book, I will lay myself on the altar of public opinion and prove to you that leaders can be restored. If you are of the opinion that mistakes and moral blowups are unpardonable when it comes to leaders, this book is going to be hard for you to read. But if you are willing to step into this unique area of ministry and life of second chances, this book will show you that there is truly an art in restoring failed leaders. As strange and foreign as the title of this book is to so many (and that's why I chose it), so also is the restoring of leaders back to full and complete roles of leadership.

I pray you enjoy the journey; I sure did.

Chapter 1

The Man behind the Pages

I thought it best for you, the reader, to get to know me before we get into any real discussions. All too often, I read books never really being able to identify with the author or whom the book is written about. I believe it is vitally important for you to know the author, or at least identify with some parts of his life. Otherwise, it's just another book telling you about some path that you can take to become successful. That is not my intention at all. I want you to find yourself in the pages of this book. I want you to strongly identify with the issue discussed in these pages. Now, I'm not sure when that will happen, but I pray somewhere in here you will discover why you picked up this book in the first place.

On December 25, 1971, after more than seventeen hours of labor, a Christmas baby was born to a seventeen-year-old mother and nineteen-year-old father. Yes, that's right! Unwed, young, and stupid kids with no idea how to raise a child. But nonetheless, I was here and born into a family that really wasn't a family at all. My grandfather had left my grandmother years before with five kids and no support. And without a father figure in place, the inevitable happened to my mother.

My mother wed my father and things seemed to be heading in the right direction, except for a few things. Things like LSD, marijuana, cocaine, and alcohol. At the age of five, I was able to roll up dollar bills as well as any adult so my parents and their friends could snort their drugs off the glass table. My vocabulary consisted of every foul word known to man. I remember being able to put on a show for all the guests of the house on how well I could curse. Parties and beer bashes were a way of life for us.

Later, the predictable thing happened. When I was around six years old, we moved from New York to Florida, where things just got worse. There was a major argument that turned violent, with my father smashing the place to pieces. I remember there being blood on the walls, with the TV literally kicked in and appliances destroyed. So, my mother left my father and we were on the move again. We had zero income and no place to live, so we lived from house to house as my mother found someone willing to put us up, with certain payments, of course.

As things began to settle down somewhat, I remember going to a private party with the Allman Brothers Band in concert. I desperately wish I could erase the images I have in my head of that party. Drugs beyond your wildest dreams and people having sex in almost every bedroom in the house are just two of those images. Yes, this was my life early on. We were living an obvious generational curse.

Later on, my mother met a man nicknamed "Boom Boom." He was widely known in those parts of Florida for being a man that believed "if you can't get along, we need to get it on." However, meeting my mother somehow seemed to slow him down a bit. They soon were married and life began to take on some normalcy, if there is such a thing. This man that I now know as my dad adopted me and gave me a life that is one of those rags-to-riches types of stories. Going from poverty to the big house is really what happened. He was one of four owners of a very successful farm machinery distributorship in Florida and Georgia. Christmas and my birthday would never be the same again. Life was good. Shortly thereafter, my uncle Jim went to a David and the Giants concert in Belleview, Florida. It moved him so much that he invited the rest of us to go and visit the church with him, and every one of us found God in the following weeks.

Not long after, we moved to Perry, Georgia, to manage the branch office there. We found a wonderful church in Warner Robins where we became extremely active and did our best to support its endeavors. After two years, we moved our place of worship to a church in Macon, where things really began to happen for me. The pastor there trained me to be a sound tech, and I played numerous instruments and really felt for the first time that I knew what living for God was all about. It was in this church that I preached my first sermon. Later on, my parents became youth pastors and did a wonderful job there. But things began to change.

Somehow, somewhere, my parents lost connection with the church. They had a disagreement with the pastor and things just unraveled from there. The argument that ensued was so brutal that my dad forbade me to ever darken the doors of U.P.C.I. church again. From there, things only got worse. I was pulled out of my Christian school and placed in a secular private school closer to home. Without the influence of church in my life, I was destined to make some really big mistakes.

It was in this school that I was introduced to moonshine for the first time. We had parties on the weekends where we stole the moonshine from one my friends' dads. We would replace it with water, and because he was such a drunk, he would never notice. By the time he got to the bottom, it was all water. Drugs galore were brought to every party, but for some reason, I never tried any of them. I would only drink. I was the greatest drunk ever. No matter how much I drank, I never had a hangover. The next morning it was like it never happened. (Much to the disgruntlement of my friends.) It was during these parties that I had my first sexual encounters, which lit another fire in my soul. Thank God for his mercy during those days.

With all this new-found freedom in my life, there was still something missing and I knew it. Without the permission of my father, I started going back to the church we left months before. God started moving in my life again and things began to come together. However, this put me at great odds with my dad, and so I had to move out on my own. Just before this move, I met the young lady who eventually became my wife. So, I moved to where she was in Augusta, Georgia, and started my ministry all over again. I attended several training seminars and classes on ministry and "how-to" types of events. All of which was wonderful and great, but did little to prepare me to battle the generational curses in my life.

On September 12, 1992, April and I were married and began our life together in ministry. How I ended up with such a talented wife I will never quite understand. Later, after our first year of marriage, we were given the surprise that our first child was on the way. Shortly after his birth, we moved to Las Vegas, Nevada, to help my in-laws in establishing a new church there. I was so excited about all the possibilities. At our first service, we had one guest in the pews and five family members on the platform. A meager beginning at best, but it was great. From there, the church grew mainly from other church folk needing a new beginning. Little did I know just how symbolic that would be for me.

I went to work for a very large firm in real estate closings and I began to prosper. However, as with any large firm, you are just a number, and after two years of faithful service, they let me go. Not willing to be put down, I landed another job with the competitors across town and things really started happening. I was making more money than ever before and I was on top of the world. But again, I was just a number, and things began to unwind. They started to cut our commissions and I was not going stand for that. So, we started our own company.

The first day we started our company, we landed an impressive contract with the local county government. Sixty days thereafter, we finished our first project with a net profit of over $114,000. That's cash in the bank, baby! I was definitely on top of my game. After our first year in business, we grossed over $385,000 in revenue. Our second year, we grossed over $865,000, and our third year we grossed over $1.2 million. Here I was, twenty-seven years old and already a millionaire by most standards. Yes, the move to Vegas was a good one.

Now, did you catch that? You probably did not. I would not have either. Let me ask you another question. Why did I go to Vegas in the first place? Oh yeah, there it is—a church plant. Well, we did start the church and my tithe and offerings went a long way in assisting that to happen. But somewhere I forgot what church and ministry was all about. I started believing that God wanted me to just make money so I could pay tithe and offering. Ministry was the last thing on my mind. Besides, I had too much traveling to do in order to keep those tithe and offering payments rolling.

In 1999, I decided to retire and sell out. We had landed over fourteen deals worth over $20 million in gross revenue, and I would personally net out $4–$8 million. Yes, life was good. Homes, cars, hunting trips, trips oversees, and forty-one consecutive days on the boat were the orders of the day. When church was over on Sunday, we headed to the lake. Never mind ministry. Our boat was conveniently named *Visitation*. World Series tickets to the tune of $1500 were easy then. Too bad the Braves lost that year.

I began to believe that all I needed to do was make money. Ministry would come next, maybe. So, what happened to me, you're wondering? You know what happened. I fell. I fell very hard. But not before I lost some things. Within a year of signing those deals worth all that money, I lost everything. Homes, cars, boats, you name it. It was all gone. Bankruptcy was inevitable. But I lost more than just things. I lost the most important part of my life. I lost my soul. I died.

Chapter 2

The Rise and Fall

At the end of the last chapter I left you hanging, stating that I died. It is true. I did. I died to myself. But before we get to that, I want to warn you about this chapter. There are things that I am going to tell you that are going to disturb you. This chapter will be a compilation of stories about me and others that might tempt you to lose respect for leaders and ministry altogether. I ask that you read this all the way through before you cast your judgments. And when you're done, read it again. You may have to read it several times before it takes root in your heart. However, I do realize this is going to be tough for you. It is going to require that you leave the box you were raised in and it is going to challenge your thinking.

It was a night I will never forget. My pastor was ministering to our church and was about midway through his sermon. Now at that time, there was a group of several young ministers that I was a part of, and we were all sitting on the platform behind our pastor. I was on the edge of my seat, with my leg bouncing up and down, totally engrossed in his words. Then all of a sudden, he turned to me and said, "Finish my message," handed me the microphone, and sat down. I was fifteen years old and my pastor was a Bible scholar, a nationally known debater on doctrinal issues, and he was telling me to finish his message. I thought I was going to choke on my tongue. At the time, I did not know what came over me, but now I know that it was none other than the anointing of the Holy Spirit. I stood up, walked to the pulpit, and began to complete his message. The church went wild. People began to praise the Lord so exuberantly that it was a rush I will never forget. Then one of the young guys in our church we had been witnessing to suddenly raised his hands in the air and God filled him with the Holy Spirit. That was my first time ever ministering to anyone in church. I never felt closer to God than I did that night. Later on, our pastor asked us to minister during a midweek service, and so on my way home after the meeting, I began to ask God to show me what I was to say. Much to my surprise, he answered me. It was as if God was sitting in the car with me as he began telling me what I was to minister on. I think I cried all the way home.

Right from beginning, I knew that God had begun what I had felt for years. That constant tugging and pulling on my heart was amazing. However, the struggles started then, too. I was away at a Georgia youth camp when my mother came and picked me up and explained to me that some things had changed. She said that our pastor and my dad had a serious disagreement and that we would not be going back to church there. At that moment, my world came crashing down. We lived thirty miles from any of my church friends, so there was no one that I could turn to for help. Let me say this right here. The whole argument was started by a misunderstanding of a conversation that was reported back to the pastor inaccurately. Feelings took precedence, and things were then said that hurt everyone involved. I am not sure that my family has ever really recovered from that day, all because gossip was allowed to be the truth and not the facts.

As I already shared with you, things only got worse for me. I was taken out of the Christian school at the church and enrolled in the local private school. This definitely did not help things. Alcohol, sex, and parties continued to increase in frequency. I was lost. I was just being introduced to the ministry and then all of the sudden my family is telling me that the ministry is what caused all the mess. Several times I asked God what I was going to do. I mean, I thought I was going to preach and minister, but here I am now not even being allowed to go to church. My world was upside down and fading fast. At this time, my relationship with my dad started to deteriorate. He was also in such a state of hurt that he was not finding room for restoration. At age fifteen I did not understand this, so I blamed him for causing all of it.

Eventually, my grades fell and school became difficult. I just could not find a place that I felt I belonged to. I tried football, basketball, track, band, and weight lifting, but it just did not work. Then came the parties, and I gained the nickname "The Freak" because I would do some of the most crazy things under the influence of alcohol. One night at a party, I climbed twenty-five feet up in a tree and jumped onto the tents below that we had set up for our party. Because of my crazy tendencies, they would almost have to tie me down to keep me from doing my skydiving routines.

My family life grew more violent. My dad and I were not getting along in the least. One night, I was in the barn on our farm and I sat there for an extreme amount of time contemplating suicide with my shotgun in my hand. I felt I had nothing else to live for. The voices in my mind were loudly telling me that this was the only way out. Well, somehow I was able to walk away that night and give it another day. A few years later, I was able to sneak back to church and make my way back to God. It wasn't long before I met my bride-to-be and things just skyrocketed for the good.

As stated earlier, we went to Las Vegas to help out with a church plant and because funds were slim, my father-in-law traveled to do contract work. This left me doing the ministering while he was away. At first, I just could not seem to get my footing. Then one night it all came together. I found that same sweet anointing that came over me in the beginning and I never looked back. The church started to grow, and people started rallying to the message. God blessed on every hand it seemed, financially, numerically and spiritually.

Eventually, it was time to move back home to Georgia. We had worked hard in Las Vegas and learned much, but we had no idea what was about to take place. Well, except for the one man that spoke with me about moving home. He stated that he felt impressed of God that this moving home would be the making of us both. He said God was going to allow things to happen that would hurt us, but would ultimately be our salvation. Now at the time, I had no clue what he was talking about, but I accepted it and thought that maybe he could have missed it some. Well, he did not.

After arriving back in Georgia, we went right to work. My wife was involved in music and I was preaching regularly. Life was good and things were getting better. We took the youth department for a season and then moved into greater ministry. Other leaders seemed to fall by the wayside, and this only left more room for advancement for the rest of us. We had reached success on all fronts. Church was good. My company was soaring. My income had never been greater. I had two houses, four cars, a boat, a Yamaha Waverunner, a wife, two kids, and a dog. I was the American dream. But something happened.

I cannot say exactly when or what it was, but somewhere I just lost the whole idea of what church was all about. I became disenchanted with the process and just completely became cold. Before long I started believing things that seemed to be crazy before, but now they made sense. Things such as divorce being okay and other related moral issues. My wife and I grew further and further apart. My wife had a problem that was new to me, obsessive compulsive disorder/behavior. Apparently, it was something that she genetically inherited from her family. The way it exhibited itself was through her spending. She was capable of spending around $10,000 per month or more on our American Express card. No matter how much I asked her to stop, she could not. Things began to go wrong for us with the business and it started failing. However, the spending did not stop. It hurt me so deeply that she would not simply stop spending and help me out. Again, I understood very little about this problem she had. So, because I was hurt and felt so betrayed by her, my commitment to her and my family eroded away. Eventually, the inevitable happened.

Now, this is the part I warned you about. Yes, I found myself in a compromising situation and followed through. I became unfaithful to my marriage, family, church, and most importantly, God. Everything that I knew was wrong before was now acceptable in my mind. Everything that I knew was right before was now wrong in my mind. I lost it! So there you have it, the rise and fall of another man who happened to be a preacher.

It was three months before I left that compromising situation. It was a series of counseling, prayer, and outright miracles that I was able to get out. But that is the story of my rise and fall. There are more stories, though. Again, brace yourself. Names and places have been omitted to protect the now innocent.

Case 1. (East meets West)
He was from the East Coast, raised in a pastor's home. He went to Bible school, where he graduated with honors. And of course, what happens at a lot of Bible schools is that he found his bride. She was perfect, musically talented and loved by everyone. They were so full of life and hope for the future, working for the greatest boss of all, Jesus Christ. Life started out with a bang, being thrust into ministry and working themselves to death. He was on a business trip with his boss and there they spent several days out on the road away from their families. In the middle of their trip one night, they ended up at a strip club. They entered that smoke-filled room where lust was legal, illicit sex was encouraged, and drinks, lap dances, and private rooms were all on the menu.

Case 2. (Best friends)
He was fifteen years old and spending the night with his friend. As he woke up, he felt the strangest thing happening to him. There was his friend, experimenting with him early that morning. He just laid there motionless, hoping it would stop. Thank goodness it did before much happened and before they both went down a road of no return.

Case 3. (Youth pastor gone bad)
He was single. He was a youth pastor at a local church in his town. His daddy was a pastor from a distant town, but things just did not work out for him to stay with his dad. So, he took the position as youth pastor and lived there at the church. Not sure really how it all happened, and it doesn't really matter, he became involved with pornagraphy that took over his life.

Case 4. (Preacher the aborntionist)
They were young and dating, he a minister and she a music leader, where they attended a rather large church in the west. They soon were engaged and all things were set. But then a surprise; she became pregnant. Yes, out of wedlock and they were leaders. It gets worse. They decided to have the baby aborted. He, the preacher, paid for it himself. No one ever knew.

Case 5. (Lady and the tramp)
He was an evangelist in the Midwest. He was anointed and was very good at praying people through to God. He was more than a talented preacher, he was an exceptional teacher. But one day while preaching a revival, the pastor's wife of the church he was visiting had other plans for him. He fell. He continued preaching that revival with many coming to know the Lord, even with the affair continuing until he left.

Case 6. (The roaming evangelist)
He was an evangelist, and it was really where he felt at home. But he became burnt out and was having to work a job that took entirely too

much of his time. He had to give up church services to please his boss and keep the income up. At the very same job, a young lady there was having marital problems and soon they became involved.

Case 7. (The dynamic compromiser)
He was a dynamic preacher and very charismatic type of guy. Everyone seemed to like him and he never met a stranger. He started a church on the East Coast. He has done well and many acknowledged him for his vigor. But somewhere, somehow, something that no one knew was there happened and began to show itself. Maybe it was the people he fellowshipped or maybe something more sinister. No matter what it was, he now found himself in a relationship that started online. Things started growing more intense until he found himself compromising every belief he had known. Yes, the pastor who taught on midweek and preached anointed messages on Sunday was now the compromiser.

Now, you are probably wondering where the part was that is supposed to make you mad. Well, that is coming. I know that you can probably think of more cases than what I have listed here that have gone the same route as these, but these are different. These have quite a different ending.

Okay, so we have seven different cases with failures of pastors, ministers, and the like. They committed some of the most awful things that leaders are just not supposed to do. We have adultery, fornication, murder, molestation, etc. Sounds like something from a prison documentary, but I promise it is not. These are real leaders who are real people with real life stories that they have lived through, and they have shared them with me. Here are the cases again in a different light. Brace yourself; this may be rough on your brain.

Case 1. (East meets West)
This man today has a beautiful daughter and loving wife. They are successfully assisting a large congregation in the West. Yes, he is an assistant pastor and she is a music director. That's right, after the fall!

Case. 2 (Best friends)
We don't know if any experimenting with the same sex ever happened again. However, this pastor's son is today pastoring a church himself, with beautiful children and a wonderful wife. Right again, even after the sin.

Case 3. (Youth pastor gone bad)
Today, this man is no longer a youth pastor, but is now the assistant pastor of one of my favorite churches in the entire world. He has two beautiful children and a passionate wife. He also is one of the best altar workers you will ever find, and became one of my best friends.

Case 4. (Preacher the aborntionist)
Today, this couple is pastoring a wonderful church in the Midwest and is greatly used by God. When she sings and he preaches, God absolutely moves with anointing upon all that hear them. Their story is absolutely crushing, and at the same time, so beautifully woven by the Lord's mercy and grace. They have a house full of children. However, God took one of them through a complicated pregnancy. And to hear him tell it, it was simply God getting back what they stole from him years earlier.

Case 5. (Lady and the tramp)
Today, this man and his wife successfully assist in the Midwest and have a wonderful business that God has blessed them with. They are passionate about the kingdom and are used in wonderful ways for his service.

Case 6. (The roaming evangelist)
Today, this man has found his way home. He and his family are back together and wonderfully peaceful. They struggle with the same things that normal couples do, but there is a rock that seems to be underneath them. They are used mightily in the gifts, and the church that they serve is lucky to have them.

Case 7. (The dynamic compromiser)
This is my favorite story. Today, this man is pastoring an exciting church. It is growing and he is evangelizing his area for the cause of Christ. However, this is the best part. Unlike some of the others, he was found out and then restored. That's right, someone found out and they restored him without going through an organizational board meeting or church board meeting to figure out what kind of punishment was viable. The fact is that I am the one who found out. I saw the online chatter and emails and it was heartbreaking. I did not get mad or bitter about it, but my heart did break.

So, what did I do? I did what the Bible instructs us to do. I restored him. Now, maybe you are wondering how someone like me can restore anyone. Well, I'll tell you. But first let's get our motivation from Scripture. Galatians 6:1 says, *Brethren, if a man be overtaken in a fault, ye which are spiritual, restore such an one in the spirit of meekness; considering thyself, lest thou also be tempted.* And this is exactly what I did.

Now, first, I found a man who had the same spirit of restoration as I did. I spoke with him on the phone and explained the circumstances and he suggested we move on this immediately. So, we met at Starbucks without this man knowing that I was coming or for what reason. For the first hour of our meeting, we sat there and simply enjoyed each other's company. However, I had already prayed that God would open the door for me to bring the issue up. Well, he answered my prayer, and as the door opened, I walked through. In meekness, I began to explain to him that I felt there was a real danger in what was happening and that his entire ministry and family were at risk. I was not accusatory, nor did I use inflammatory remarks to degrade him and speak down to him. I simply let him know that I, too, had been in his shoes and all of this could end much differently than my personal situation. I simply let him know that I was aware of his situation and I wanted to help him. He accepted. From that day forward, this man's life has been changed. He did not have to go through a board scrutiny, embarrassment, or humiliation. In the privacy of the three of us and comfort of friends who truly loved him, he was restored. The biggest factor in all of this, of course, is the fact that he was willing to confess and come clean and that he wanted help. If you don't want out, then there is nothing that man or God can do.

Now let's go back to Galatians. It begins "if someone is overtaken in a fault." The fact is that every one of us at some time or another has been overtaken in a fault, right? Now, please don't go and get all philosophical on me and try to water down what a fault is. *All have sinned and come short of the glory of God* (Romans 3:23). *If we say that we have no sin, we deceive ourselves, and the truth is not in us* (1 John 1:8). Sin is sin no matter who commits it or what it is they commit. If you lie, cheat, or steal, it is sin. If you cut someone off in traffic because they aggravated you with their driving skills, then it is sin to you. *To Him that knoweth to do good and doeth it not, to him it is sin* (James 4:17). Okay, now that we know that everyone has sinned, let's get into what we are to do with that information.

When a person has sinned, our passage tells us that *we which are spiritual* —Did you see that? It says that we which are spiritual should restore the folk who have fallen into sin. There are several ways we can take this, but one that I just love is that if you will not restore a person, then you are not very spiritual. The other is that if you are going to restore a person who has fallen, then you must be spiritual to be able to accomplish the task. For all the Bible scholars out there, this is what it says in the Greek: *4152 Pneumatikos a, GK: 4461 [- 4154], spiritual, pertaining to the Spirit; (n.) Spiritual person* (Strong's). If *spiritual* means that which pertains to the Spirit, then it only stands to reason that if we are spiritual, then restoring people will be something that we do without thinking because His spirit lives inside of us.

Restoration is not an easy subject. There are all kinds of issues that remain out there on the fringes. However, we will deal with some of that in the chapters to come. Galatians goes on to say that we are to *restore* them. Here is the Greek again: *2675 v. GK: restore kataartizo. to restore, put in order, mend; to make complete, equip, train; to prepare, ordain:-perfect, make perfect, mending, fitted, framed, perfected, perfectly joined together, prepared, restore* (Strong's). I don't think that it takes a rocket scientist to figure out where this is going. I have a scriptural mandate that says that I am to restore or perfect my brother or sister when they sin. If I take judgment on them, ostracize, ban, and isolate them because of the fall they have taken, then I have not followed Scripture. It is my duty as a child of God to help complete them in their journey.

Let me ask you: What was Jesus' ministry all about? Was it not restoration? You may say that he was restoring a world that was lost and did not know it. Really? What about the fact that he told the women that he actually came for the house of Israel (the saved folk) and did not have time to fool around with dogs (Matthew 15:26, Mark 7:27, emphasis mine)? The fact is that he came to save that which was lost no matter how they got there, who they were, or even if they were of the house of Israel; they still needed his restoration. You may say that we do restore them but they will never lead people again. I say that you are wrong! Not only will they lead, but they now have a better grip on leadership and will be more effective as leaders. Why was Jesus so effective? Because, in all points, he was tempted just you like you and me. The only difference, which is a big one, is the fact that he was without sin.

So, we have a God who knows our feelings when we are tempted, and in case we do fall, he has the ability, through his blood, to restore us. And because we are ambassadors of his gospel, we must preach the message of restoration, no matter when it is needed. Now, in no way or form am I saying that you must fall to be effective. If you never fall into some of the more despicable sins, I congratulate you and thank God for you. You are a true witness that it can be done. However, if you do not get the message of restoration in your heart and have compassion on those who do fall and take on the heart of Christ, then maybe you have fallen already.

Now my story

It was a long road back. I did not preach or speak publicly for about three years, not because I did not have opportunity, but because I was incredibly wounded. When I resigned from my position at the church, publicly no less, it rocked everyone's world. Although I never said what I did when I resigned, speculation started rumors that were unbelievably inaccurate. Before long, the church board forced a meeting that was designed not only to have me removed and excommunicated from the church, but was also designed to take out the pastor as well. You see, he was a man that believed in restoration. The board and some members of the church knew it, so they gunned for him as well. But it is amazing to see that the very ones who headed up the execution party were the ones who had grown up in an era where they were taught to execute their leaders should they fall and make a mistake. They were taught that this gospel is only good for sinners coming to Christ, but is of no real value to Christians who need it after the day of salvation. Why would anyone think this way? It is because there is a philosophy that is unwritten but impressed within the recesses of our belief system—that salvation is an event or destination. How far could we be from the truth? Salvation is a journey that one must travel day in and day out. When you take a journey, there are many different roads to take. Some roads are easier than others. Some are scenic and some are treacherous. Some roads will take us places we never intended to go. However, the best part is that once we realize we have taken the wrong road we don't have to stay there, we can get back on the right route.

It was at a revival service that I was in, and we were at the altar when I noticed one of the men who had a part in my trial at the church board meeting standing close by. I went over to him, hugged him, buried my head into his chest, and I prayed with tears asking God to forgive not him but me. I asked God to forgive me for ever letting this man down and taking for granted our friendship. I asked God to lay no charge to his life because of me. Understand, until this point, our relationship was not good. We were at odds and I was somewhat bitter for his involvement. But that day, something happened that I cannot explain. As I prayed that prayer, it was as if God erased the past for both of us. I walked away that day with the feeling that everything that I had done and everything that I had suffered was now truly under the blood of Christ.

I left there that day to go on and pastor a great church in Jefferson County, Georgia, where God did some incredible things. We took a church of fifteen and raised it to about sixty (in a town of just under three hundred residents) and watched God produce several miracles inside that little country church. Yes, that is right. All this happened after a fall. Also, remember I told you that my wife had a serious issue herself. Today, she has completely recovered. She walks daily with Christ as he guides her through the thorn in her flesh. Yes, she still to this day deals with the compulsive behavior that robbed her of life. But because of a pastor that believed she was worth restoring, today she is extremely successful in her music ministry. She has had the opportunity to work with some of the best and has been privileged to record in the studio a few times. However, through it all, what she learned is invaluable. She has replaced her compulsive need to spend with a need to worship Christ.

A great friend of mine, Rodney Baker, said this about my ministry: "Before you went through the fire, your preaching was polished and given to excellent speech." He said, "You were good. But now, after the fall, your preaching is not only polished, but now it is wrapped in passion and that of a man that knows he has been given a second chance."

The Case for Restoration

Chapter 3

A Second Time

Have you ever been given a second chance? I know this seems like a rhetorical question, but I am really not trying to be smart about it. Really though, have you? Right about now you are thinking back to some wild, strange time in your life when, yes, you were given that second chance. However, the fact is that we all have been given that second chance, third chance, fourth chance and, well, you get the picture. Not one of us can claim having never made a mistake. Therefore, we all have been given that second chance. I believe it is correct to say that this is really what Christ's ministry was and is all about—second chances.

Do you remember those times in your life and the feeling that you had when you realized just how close you came to buying it? I remember times when I just knew it was all over for me. Times like when I was shining rabbits in Georgia. (That is night hunting with a spotlight, which is highly illegal for those of you who never venture outdoors.) As we made our way down an old fence row, a pair of headlights turned on and came straight for us. Yep, it was the state wildlife game warden. I flipped out, stomped the gas, and tried to make my escape. Problem was I tried to do it without headlights on so he could not see us and I ran slap into the ditch. Of course, the truck was stuck and here we were, me and my best friend, screaming at the top of our lungs, saying, "We are going to jail. Oh my god, we are going to jail." The truth of the matter is that I think I wet my pants that night. Well, by the grace of God, we got the truck out of the ditch and we finally made our escape. We got our second chance that night, and I do not remember ever trying to spotlight rabbits again.

The book of Jonah in the Bible is among the shortest books written, but is chock-full of life application for leaders. The first chapter opens with, *Now the word of the Lord came to Jonah.* Pretty serious stuff if you ask me. Whenever God speaks, you better take a moment and listen. God tells Jonah that he needs to go to the great city of Nineveh and teach a few Bible studies. However, Jonah has other plans. He wants absolutely nothing to do with Nineveh. In fact, he goes the other way. Oh, did I mention that Jonah was a prophet? Yepper, he was. He was God's man, and going "AWOL." He heads for Tarshish, buys a one-way ticket, and boards a boat. The Scripture tells us that God sent out a great wind. Remember this in a moment. There are some really serious implications here. So the ship is nearly beat to pieces and everyone is now looking at Jonah. They now know he has blown it, and he knows he has blown it. So he does what any self-respecting leader would do in a moral blowup—he commits suicide. Just kidding. But really, that is what he tried to do. So they throw his backsliding carcass into the sea. But before they do, they have a little revival on the boat and the men are all saved right then and there and make vows unto God. Doesn't that strike you as funny? Here is a totally rebellious leader and he has a small revival just before his attempted suicide, and when he is overboard, they make vows to God. Sometimes these stories just blow my mind. Anyway, on we go.

The last verse in chapter one of Jonah says that the Lord prepared a great fish. Some say a whale, some say a rather large fish, but it really does not matter, so let's just say that it was a whale of a fish.

Hey, it could have been a megalodon shark. Laugh if you will, but whales don't normally eat people, and besides, Craig Groschell said it. Again, hold on to this. God prepared the fish. Now after three days and three nights of being nothing more than big fish bait, Jonah decides it is a good idea to pray. That really shows just how messed up he really was. Three days of living in puke and he will not repent. There are so many sermons in this little book, you could preach for hours.

So Jonah finally ends up on the beach like yesterday's lunch. He stinks, he is probably bleached ghostly white due to the acids in the stomach of the big fish he lived in, and he is obviously just hanging around. I am not sure if he thinks this was just a really wild Caribbean vacation or what, but he is just sitting on the beach chilling out and trying to dissipate some of that stench when God speaks. Chapter three opens with: *And the word of the Lord came to Jonah a second time.* So God comes to him a second time and gives the exact same orders as before. So here we have a man of God who committed the most awful thing a God-called man can do, be disobedient, and God gives him a second chance. The leader, the preacher who without doubt did not deserve a second chance gets a do over. So what does this mean for you and me? Simply, God will and does give messed up leaders a second chance.

Need more proof? Let's start from Genesis and move forward, but we will only pick up the more notable characters for sake of time and page space. Adam and Eve sinned against God, ran from God, and then when given opportunity to fess up, lied to God by throwing off on each other, and then ultimately blamed Satan. This was the first "the devil made me do it" scenario. Noah drinks too much of his own wine and ends up streaking around in his birthday suit, and then after the matter, lives on for another three hundred plus years. What about Abraham and Sarah, the forerunners of faith? God gives them his word of promise and they doubt, laugh, and take matters into their own hands. Abraham, with the consent of Sarah, sleeps with another woman just in case God got it wrong, and yet Abraham and

Sarah are patriarchs of our faith and we are their spiritual seed. Jacob proves to be a liar and a deceiver and yet has an encounter with God that changes his name and the people of God from his generation on. Then there are Joseph's brothers who sold him to Egypt and still got their second chance because of a brother's love. Moses, trying to be a leader, kills a man and then rises up as the greatest leader of Israel's history. Sampson loses out and then gets his second chance and does more to free Israel during his moment of death than all the previous years of his life. King David, the dysfunctional father, adulterer, murderer, and lackadaisical rebellious leader who, after all is said and done, is known as a man after God's own heart.

Again, for the sake of time, let's jump to the New Testament. Now the most famous disciple of them all, Peter, a loud mouth, cursing, and impetuous sailor who always liked to stir things up, preaches the first Pentecostal message after denying Christ not once, not twice, but "three times a lady." I mean, denies Christ three times. John Mark, who Paul kicks out of the church and tries to kick out of the ministry, is redeemed by Barnabas. Later, Paul states in Scripture for us that he *is* profitable for the ministry. I do not know what John Mark did to tick off Paul, but it had to be really bad, because he spoke of himself as the biggest sinner of all and then later tells the world and beyond that John Mark was "the man."

For anyone to say that once a leader blows it badly that they cannot or should not be allowed a second chance is beyond me. The Bible is chock-full of examples of where the letter of the law should have applied, but the greater principles of mercy and grace were applied. If you are one of those who believes that these leaders do not deserve a second chance, then why are you still in ministry? Why are you still in leadership? Look back over your life and pick out the areas where you messed it up and ask yourself the question, why am I still here? The reason is because whether you realized it at the time or not, you were given a second chance. Someone somewhere gave you, a messed up leader, a second chance to redeem yourself. Sure, you look at it now and with distance from the event, you may not feel that it was really that big of deal, but truth be known, there was someone out there during that event that wanted your head on a platter. But thank God for a man or woman of God that refused to allow you to be thrown away!

The trap we get into is that we put levels on sin and mistakes. This very statement opens a neat discussion though. I can hear the questions now: so what about a person who murders his neighbor? Is that not a stronger level of sin than someone who, let's say, steals? Sure it is. Again, you have got to avoid the trap. Here is my opinion on the matter. There are without doubt levels of consequence for different sins or unlawful acts. Those levels have been established by the founding leadership of our country, and frankly, the world. However, does murder disqualify a person from being used of God any more than someone who steals? Does the sin of theft disqualify a person from being used of God any more than the person who gossips? Proverbs 6:16–19 lays it out for us. It says that there are six things that God hates. Yet there are seven that are an abomination to him. Here is the list, in order: pride, lying, murder, evil thoughts, tendency to run to evil, false witness, and sowing discord among the people.

The way I read this is that if you commit any of those listed offenses, you are as contrary to God at that moment as you will ever be. So God, based on this verse, states that gossip (discord) is as bad as murder to him. Have you ever gossiped? Of course you have; everyone has at some point in his life. With that being declared, should you resign from your church? Should you resign from your position of leadership? If we live according to this Scripture and not of what we currently believe disqualifies leadership, then yes, you should.

We think for some reason that gossip is not as bad as murder. But God does not agree with us. Another question I hear a lot is what about an "eye for an eye"? That's an easy one. We now live in the dispensation of grace. We now live after the events on the cross.

There is not a sin out there than cannot be forgiven now that His blood has been shed for a ransom. Sure, the consequence in this life may be hard to deal with and you may go to jail and serve your time, but who says you cannot preach to someone while there? Where does it say in the Bible that you cannot "lead" someone to Christ after the sin? Is that not what leading or leadership is really all about anyway, leading people to Christ? The essence of all leadership is in leading others to God.

A few paragraphs ago, I told you to remember a couple of things. One is that God prepared the storm. The other is that God also prepared the fish. The storm and the fish were both prepared and sent by God. The sins of Jonah were disobedience and prejudice of another people. But not one person knew what was in his heart until God sent a prepared storm and prepared situation (fish) to swallow him whole. The failures that we see leadership go through and succumb to are not the core sins in their life. There is a much deeper issue inside of them. The things we see unveil themselves in the lives of failed leaders are only symptomatic of an inner core sin, and God has purposely prepared some serious public issues to arrest them. Nothing will arrest the leadership abilities of anyone quicker than public failure.

But the fact is this: Jonah did go on to finish the ministry that God called him to. Nineveh experienced revival and the city was saved for that time. Jonah got his second chance and used it well. I urge you to change your thinking if you feel second chances are not for failed leaders. I beg of you to change. If not, you may need to walk ever so softly; you just may be the next Jonah we hear about.

Chapter 4

Three Is a Crowd

Just in case you need support for the previous chapters, I have written this one. There is a mystery about the Gospel that, if you really think about it, completely defies understanding. Anyone, male or female, rich or poor, ugly or beautiful, is accepted as they are by God. The greatest thing about the Gospel is that I do not have to measure up before I come to know him. In fact, I don't ever have to measure up because I never will. *But we are all as an unclean thing, and all our righteousnesses are as filthy rags* (Isaiah 64:6). Everything we try and do to be clean is a futile attempt to make ourselves good enough for heaven. How great is that kind of love that God did it all for me. For God so loved the world that he gave … It never said that we reached some level of his approval, then he shed his blood for us. He did it before we were ever even born. That is a very hard thing for you and I to grasp today. We size up everyone we meet, and based on some mythical scale of measurement, we decide within minutes of making someone's acquaintance whether or not they will exist in our little world. Not so with the Lord. Truly, His grace is still amazing.

To prove this point, I want to direct your attention to Luke, chapter fifteen. This entire chapter is dedicated to the revelation that "all have sinned and come short of the glory of God." There are three parables that Jesus uses in this chapter to prove his love for you and me. First, it is worthy to note the setting in which he exposes this revelation. He is sitting with those who the Pharisees view as sinners. You know, the unworthy folk who they believe just flat out miss the mark. And appropriately so, they condemn him for fellowshipping with such ruthless people.

The first parable Jesus uses is that of the lost sheep. I like to call this the parable of the lost saint. Sheep, as well as saints, cannot survive without their Shepherd. They will find themselves lost unless they receive direction. Romans 10:14 states very clearly that we cannot survive without the preacher. In other words, we will get lost. Not dealing well with being called a sheep? You need to read Isaiah 53:6 again. *All we like sheep have gone astray; we have turned every one to his own way.* Yep, we all get lost. Sorry, but it is in the Bible.

But! Jesus tells them that he leaves the ninety-nine and searches for the one who lost its way. He is so intent on not losing one that he leaves the righteous and goes to find that one sheep that did not intend on getting lost, but did. He goes so far as to say that all of heaven rejoices more over that one sheep coming back home than all the righteous posturing of those still within the confines of the church. You need to think about this one a bit. It will eventually come to you. We will write more on this later, in another chapter.

The second parable Jesus uses is that of the lost coin. I have named this one as the parable of a lost world. A young lady who has ten silver coins has lost one. She lights a lamp and sweeps the floor until she finds it. And as heaven rejoices over one lost sheep returning home, she also rejoices for finding the valuable coin. Notice Jesus refers to the coin as being silver, meaning he placed value on it even though it was lost. The reason I named this parable as the parable of a lost world is because just as the coin does not know it is lost, neither does the world. They are simply doing what has come naturally to them and cannot realize their situation.

That is the trickery of sin. You can be lost and think that you know where you are going. Yet, every night and every day of your life, you hear that ever so tiny, though consistent, voice telling you that there is more to life than just living and that you really do not know where you stand. As the world turns, the reality splashes the front pages of every newspaper in our land that our world really is lost and they don't know it. However, the lost in this case can do nothing about it. They must be found! We must sweep our communities, schools, shopping malls, and workplaces to find that which is so valuable to him. As the coin simply laid there in its dark, recessed corner until it was found, our world will only do the same until we sweep over them in love and compassion, pick them up, dust them off, and place them in their God-desired place of valuables. As Christians, we must stop looking at people as less than. We must get back to the basics that Christ died for "whosoever will." As a person, I am no better than the corrupt banker, lawyer, doctor, or town drunk in my community. I am no better than the crack whore in my town. I am no better than the narcotics dealer selling his product. My worth to Christ is not one cent more than any other human being on this earth. Don't think so? Tell me this. When people die, what happens to their bodies? They are buried like everyone else before them and like everyone else that follows them. That's right, simply buried. Although your casket may cost more than some, your body will do the same in a $10,000 casket or $1500 pine box; it will vanish away sooner or later. As our great forefathers are often quoted in the annals of history as saying, "all men are created equal."

You may say that you understand that, but do you really express it with the way you live your life? A list of these facts was recently uncovered by a survey conducted by the Barna Group. A majority of outsiders (people not in church), 57 percent, say Christians are quick to find faults with others. A large number of outsiders, 51 percent, believe that churches are not loving environments. You may say that you are not judging others and devaluing them, but the message is getting lost. If somehow we can wake to the realization that Christ values all, regardless of what they have done, who they are, or where they come from, we might actually save a few more before Christ's return.

The third parable that Jesus uses is that of the prodigal son. I like to call this one the parable of the purposely "gone bad" minister. I do realize it can be used for all people, regardless of their use in the kingdom, but for the sake of this chapter we will call him a preacher. We have a young man full of life, living in his father's house. For whatever reason, he decides that he wants his reward (inheritance) now, before it is appropriate to receive. He purposely leaves home and commits his awful acts. The story quickly rushes through to the point of his demise. Not much here to tell, I guess. The fall rarely takes long and usually the story is brief. When you think of it, does it ever really take that long for us to mess things up in our lives? No doubt. After a famine descended on the country of his choosing, the preacher finally finds himself in a pigpen, eating the very things he most likely preached about in his sermons. The very things he told countless others to avoid, he, the preacher, finds himself right smack in the middle of it.

As you know, he comes to his senses and realizes that at his father's house there is plenty to eat. He says it like this: *that even the hired servants have enough food and to spare.* Now notice something. He finally gets it right. He realizes for the first time that he is no better than the servants. In fact, he would glory in being one of them. Let me now say this to all ministers: *You are nothing more than a servant and never will be more than a servant.* So stop acting like something more and do what you have been called to do; serve God's people!

The prodigal preacher makes his way back home and before he can get there, the father sees him coming and rushes out to meet him. We have all heard every sermon imaginable preached on this, but it is amazing to me that the father was looking for his lost preacher the whole time. The father then meets him there. Where? A long way off. When he does, he gives him a kiss of acceptance. We could stand to learn a lot from this parable if we should be so brave. The father never scolded him, never shamed him, never put him down, but simply kissed him and welcomed him back into the house. He put the robes of honor back on him and placed authority back on his finger. He restored everything back to him. They killed the fatted calf that they had been preparing, and I love what the New Living Translation version says here, *so the party began.*

But wait! There is a problem. The other preacher in the house is not so happy about it. In fact, he is downright stirred up with righteous indignation. He can't believe that this is going on. His is fit to be tied! He questions his father about it, but I do not believe he understands what he told him. The story never depicts whether or not the son went to the party and he probably did not. There is an interesting nugget of truth in the reasoning he gave the elder son, though. He told him that he had always been with him and everything the father had was his already. He could have thrown a party at any time. But he did not. What is the message here? The elder son was so worried about his brother getting what he did not deserve or getting what he did deserve that he failed to enjoy the blessings that the father had already made for his own disposal. When we get so interested in making sure that someone is punished for whatever wrongs they commit, we will miss out on the very opportunity that God has afforded us and we will not even recognize it. One more thing can be gleaned here. The elder son was more interested in his brother's death than he was in his renewed life. If the story could go on, I believe we would read of the ultimate failure of the elder brother, the failure of his heart. He could not carry on the business of his father when his heart was so far from him. However, you can believe that the prodigal preacher knew well the father's heart, because he experienced it. I believe he lived the rest of his days making sure that everyone knew well the heart that accepts the prodigal.

The title of this chapter says it all. The entire chapter of Luke 15 is dedicated to every facet a person can identify with when it comes to being lost. Three is a crowd because the evidence is so overwhelming. Three stories with three different scenarios of how they were lost but the end was the same. Complete restoration every time, no matter what. God is in the business of restoration. Shouldn't we be about our father's business?

Chapter 5

Modern Day Lazaruses

In the book of John, chapter 11 is the story of Lazarus that we all have heard so many times that well, it's just another story to most, unfortunately. As common as this story has become within the halls of our religious buildings, I believe it was a chapter written exclusively for today's church concerning its leadership. It was not written for the sinner or lost soul before they come to know Christ. It was not written to prove the resurrecting power of Christ, because that proof would come later in his own resurrection. But it was written for detailed directions on how the church should handle its failed leadership.

The implication given in this Scripture is that Jesus and Lazarus were the best of friends. I bet you never thought of Jesus having best friends, did you? Well, he did, unless I am missing it here. The news came that Lazarus was at death's door, and Jesus was being asked to come and do his thing. He makes a completely wild and out-of-place statement. It almost sounded like one of the religious clichés we use today. "This situation is not for the purpose of death, but is going to be for the glory of God and that Jesus might [get a little kudos on the side]," (emphasis mine). However, Jesus did not move or do anything; he just sat there. This was highly unusual activity for the one who has up until this point healed and rebuked every sickness that came to him. Nonetheless, he did not move.

After two days, Jesus decided to go and visit Lazarus and while on the way, he then tells his disciples that Lazarus is asleep. A sigh of relief passes through their thinking, that all is well with Lazarus, and then Jesus has to go a bit further and tells them that no, he really has bought it. He's dead. Then he says the strangest thing: "and I am glad that I was not there to stop it, but nevertheless, let's go," (emphasis mine). Then Thomas, moved with emotion, is all for going to see the body, but also adds he wants to die with Lazarus. I don't know about you, but that is just one of those statements that everyone could live without. I really just don't get why that piece was included in there. Anyway, let us move on.

Jesus arrives and he figures out that Lazarus has been buried for four days at this point. Martha hears that Jesus is in town and she runs out to him and gives Jesus a scolding. "If only you had been here before he died, you could have saved him," (emphasis mine). Now, first we must understand the setting that Jesus intended for us to imagine here. First of all, you need to remember that Jesus said this "sickness was not unto death, but for the glory of God." Secondly, sickness is symbolic of corruption. The sickness in this case was being used to show us in the natural world what has really taken place spiritually. Our bodies are corruptible, and Jesus was allowing the science experiment of this sickness to demonstrate a higher principle that he was trying to get across. Again, Martha makes the statement, "If only you had been here." You see, she believed Jesus could have healed her brother, but she does not believe that Jesus can raise him from the dead. She believes the resurrection will happen one day, but not now. Mary, a few verses later, also has virtually the same conversation with him. So, even though they sent for Jesus to come and heal him, after he dies they simply bury him. Basically, it's too late to fix things now. No going back; he is in the tomb of corruption and nothing else can be done. He is finished.

Jesus asked to see the place where they laid him and when he arrives there, Jesus cries. The tears that Jesus cries are known as the shortest verse of Scripture in the entire Bible, yet it is the most meaningful to the church today. Hold that thought. He then asked for the stone to be rolled away and the protests were deafening. He stinks! He smells! That situation is already dead, God, and we just can't bear to bring that situation back in the open.

This is exactly what the church does today. We bury our dead ministries. We bury our fallen leaders. They become sick (corrupted) in some sort of situation and lose their way, lose their integrity, and it seems there is nothing we can do, so they die. And all we can do and all we believe that can be done is to bury them and forget about it. Oh we believe that God can stop a sickness (situation) before it really happens, but we refuse to believe that God can raise a ministry back to its former glory after a sinful fall. We protest in near agony of the thought that someone's ministry can be brought back to life after corruption. So we do the only thing that has been done for years; we bury them and never allow them to live again. We wrap them up in grave clothes and try to put spices on them so the situation won't smell too badly. We bury them behind boulders of closure so we can move on with our church boards and ministry boards so as to forget what happened and restore faith in our belief systems. They become our modern-day Lazaruses. Jesus weeps at the gravesite not because he was sad for Lazarus, but I believe because he peered into the future and he saw all the Lazaruses that would suffer behind boulders, grave clothes, and spices to cover up their failures and be buried. So the question is what can we do? What are we supposed to do? The answers lie within the story still.

Again, when Jesus arrives at the tomb, the first thing he does is command the people to roll the stone away. Secondly, he calls for Lazarus to come forth. Thirdly, he commands the people to let him loose and let him go. The only thing that the church is responsible for is rolling the stone away and loosing the grave clothes and allowing them to be set free. That's all you have to do. Stop covering the situations and stop trying to bury ministries and leaders that fail. Roll the stones away and take the grave clothes off of them. They're not dead; they are just waiting to be called forth again. Jesus gave the word for Lazarus to come forth because the calling is God's responsibility, not ours. Romans 11:29 tells us that the gifts and calling of God are without repentance, meaning they are irrevocable. Once God calls them back, all you have to do is allow them to be set loose.

How many leaders do you know that have been buried and not allowed to function within roles of leadership because of a terrible mistake? There are thousands, and I am sure we could find them all across this country and the world. If there was ever a chapter written for the church today, it is the eleventh chapter of John. Kind of an eleventh hour message, maybe? I am sure there are some that take exception with what is written here. That's okay; they have the right to be wrong and make the same mistake as did the Pharisees of that day. Immediately following the restoration of Lazarus, they held a board meeting to discuss this bringing back to life a man (ministry) that was dead. They were not all too happy about it, and in fact, they wanted to kill Jesus from that day forward. Isn't it interesting how bringing someone back to life is what took the Pharisees over the edge and is what started the plotting to kill Jesus? Think about it. In Chapter twelve, they even plotted to kill Lazarus himself. They simply wanted to kill the evidence that proves you can live again after corruption. But the truth be known, there will be fellow ministers and leadership within your sphere of influence that will also want to take you out if you follow Jesus' example on this. You will experience more criticism than you ever have if you dare roll the stones away and cut away the grave clothes of a fallen comrade. But I beg of you, please roll the stones away; there are so many that God wants to call forth back to life.

I want to bring to light one more thought from the chapter we have been writing about here. Jesus allowed Lazarus to die. He had the power to stop it, delay it, but he did not. He allowed the whole drama to unfold before he even made any movement toward the situation. I know he said that it would be for the glory of God and to glorify his son (speaking of himself), but I want to delve further into this glory thing. No one would normally think that death could be a glorifying thing. I know, the Scripture says that the passing of a saint is a good thing, but normally we just don't view death through those glasses. We actually spend our entire lifetimes trying to avoid and prolong the inevitable meeting with death. The coinciding part of this is that we do that in the spiritual as well. Death is not a subject we like to take on. If you have ever been to a wake or funeral, you can witness the somewhat awkward moment as people look for the words to say to each other but can't seem to get it out. Words almost seem unfitting. Nothing we say makes the family or friend of the deceased feel any better about it. To be frank about it, death sucks! But again, we all will face it someday.

Earlier we compared the sickness of Lazarus to corruption. He was corrupted physically, so therefore his body was dying. Again, this is symbolic of what takes place in a person when they become spiritually corrupted. James 1 says that when lust has conceived, it brings sin, and sin brings death. Now, Jesus stated that this would be for the glory of God and his son, so there had to be some underlying message here. May I submit to you that it is the message that death brings? Once death occurred in the body of Lazarus, whatever his illness was also died with him. By death, the corruption also died. So in the spiritual, unless death takes place, the corruption lives on. Please understand, I am not saying that we must die in order to be forgiven. Jesus' blood takes care of the forgiveness and covering of sin. What I am trying to relay here is that whatever it was that caused the leader to fail must die, and in order for that to happen, the leader must die out to himself.

Think about it. What causes leaders to fail? Don't name the symptoms of the issue, but what is the core infection? It is pride. Leaders fail because of pride. Nothing more and nothing less. So, by allowing Lazarus to buy it, he also took out the corruption. Once this was complete, he called Lazarus back to life. So, when a leader blows it and blows it badly, there will and must be a death—the death of their pride. Once this is accomplished, and if the church will roll away the stone, God will then call them forth again. Then it is up to the church to set them free and allow the anointing to cover them again. So here we have a partnership. The leader ridding himself of pride through death, and the church doing what the church is called to do; restoring our modern-day Lazaruses.

Chapter 6

God Does Not Believe in Divorce

You are probably wondering what in the world the title of this chapter has got do with anything already written in this book. Well, now that I have your attention, let's proceed. It is no secret that the divorce rate among men and women is near the highest that it has ever been. I cannot give an exact statistic because of the fluctuation from year to year, but suffice it to say that it hovers around 60 percent for couples married five years or less. There are all kinds of reasons as to why, but that is not really important unless someone is willing to take the blame. Most don't.

We live in a world where people have little to no commitment in their lives. We change jobs, homes, and cars every couple of years. We change computers every six months and cell phones every thirty days or so. Okay, I stretched the last one a bit, but I think you get my drift. We are not a people that understand commitment in the least. Again, who is to blame? I am not sure, but I think the church has had a large part in it. Ouch, I know! That is quite an accusation, but I will explain in a moment.

In the Jewish community back in the days of old, the act of marriage was a really big deal. In fact, the whole idea was started with a contract. For the sake of history and stressing just how important this was to the Jews and God himself, I will give a good deal of detail. Jewish families would often get together and create a contract that was binding on both sides. They would basically speak for their children and marry them off by contract long before they had any kind of decision-making capability. The fathers would get together and create the terms of this contract. Once the groom and perspective bride came of age, they would become engaged and the groom would return with his father back to his house where he would instruct the groom on creating his little mansion. This little mansion was a room, an extension, right off the side of his father's house. The father was the one who decided when the construction was completed. Once completed, the groom, along with the best man, would take the most popular route in town, blowing a trumpet to alert his bride that he was coming. Let's not forget that the bride was also preparing herself with a wedding gown from material provided by the groom during the construction of the little mansion.

The bride would meet the groom in the street and begin their journey to the place of the marriage ceremony. They would not recite vows, but simply read the contract that was created all those years before. They would recite this contract in the presence of all and then make their way to the little mansion. There, with the best man just outside the door, the consummation of the marriage would take place. After the act of marriage was completed, the groom would step outside so the best man could witness the blood-stained sheets proving that the bride was in fact pure. This was a big deal to the Jewish culture. If it was witnessed that she was not pure, Jewish law allowed the groom to immediately consider the marriage null and void. The next day, he would go to the court and have the annulment put in place. There was also a great possibility that the bride would be stoned and her family disgraced forever.

Now, in accordance with the title of this chapter, I still state for the record: *GOD DOES NOT BELIEVE IN DIVORCE.* That's right. I said it. God does not believe in it, and it goes completely against His will when it is allowed. Just so you do not think I am off my rocker here, let's read some Scripture. In Matthew 19, around verse 3, the Pharisees came to him and were doing what they did most of the time concerning Jesus. They were trying to trap him against what is written in the Word of God. They wanted to know how he felt about divorce. *And he answered and said, Have ye not read, that he who made them from the beginning made them male and female, and said, For this cause shall a man leave his father and mother, and shall cleave to his wife; and the two shall become one flesh? So that they are no more two, but one flesh. What therefore God hath joined together, let not man put asunder* (Matthew 19:4–7). In verse 7, the Pharisees quickly shot back that Moses said it was okay to give a "bill of divorcement."

Jesus, being the quick and all-knowing God that he is, offered this convicting statement back as his answer: *He saith unto them, Moses for your hardness of heart suffered you to put away your wives: but from the beginning it hath not been so. And I say unto you, Whosoever shall put away his wife, except for fornication, and shall marry another, committeth adultery: and he that marrieth her when she is put away committeth adultery* (Matthew 19:8–9). Did you see it? Jesus himself, at the end of verse 8, says, "but from the beginning it hath not been so." Divorce has not been and will never be God's desire, design, or excuse for anyone. However, we in the church still divorce over all kinds of issues, including adultery.

So, think about it. How many people in your church have divorced over the last few years? I am sure the numbers may be staggering. In almost every situation where divorce takes place, it is over issues that the couple can't seem to get over or forgive and forget. Divorce is the final act of calling it quits and saying that this situation cannot and will not be corrected and fixed. It is, in fact, the ultimate statement of *un-forgiveness*. It actually is un-forgiveness that lives on into eternity. If I divorce my spouse, I am saying that I am not committed to you any longer, and therefore I break that commitment with this act. I am also stating that whatever led me here to this decision is so bad that I cannot and will not forgive you for it. That is a tough statement, I know, and you may not like it, but it is the truth. It will probably have to roll around in your mind for awhile, but I believe you will get it eventually.

Before I continue, let me state for the record that there are some situations out there that may not fit within this area, such as abuse, both physical and mental. I am not a supporter of anyone putting up with that kind of stuff. However, leaving the situation and divorce are different things. You must protect yourself and those that you love, but at the same time, you have a personal responsibility to remain righteous and pure until that offending spouse gives you the bill of divorce. A very deep subject for another book.

So, back to what God thinks about it. Again, Jesus himself states that, from the beginning, this kind of thing was never intended by God, and a flawed leader (Moses) fell under the weight of pressure of those he led and allowed it. God is not a god that begins something then changes his mind. *I am the Lord and I change not...* (Malachi 3:6). God is huge on commitment. *No man putting his hand to the plow and looks back is fit for the kingdom* (Luke 9:26). God is not an "on again and off again" type of God. If he says it, he means it. Can you imagine if God decided that all that stuff on the cross was just a bit too much for a people who didn't seem to care anyway, so his stripes no longer mean healing for his people? Or what if you strove all your life to live for him, and God decides to change the rules after you die and states that you no longer qualify for eternal life with him? Have you ever played a game with someone that changed the rules throughout the game? Do you remember the frustration you felt? Oh I do and all I wanted to do was beat that kid into the ground. For the record, I did not. However, I did stop playing the game.

I stated earlier that I felt the church had something to do with the ever-rising divorce rate. Let me now clarify my statement. We witness to people all day long throughout our busy lives and we tell them at every church service that Jesus forgives and forgets, that there is nothing you can do short of blasphemy that will keep him from loving you and using you for his glory. However, let a leader and preacher make a mistake, you know, one of those big ones, and it's on like Donkey Kong. So with the very same people watching how we handle failed leaders, we expect them to believe us when we say that there is nothing you can do to be treated like this failed leader except be a failed leader. I am sorry, but that just does not make sense. Leaders are people, too. Preachers are people, too. The same forgiveness and the same blood of Christ cover us all.

God is a God of constants. He never changes and he never changes the rules of the game. If he called you to be a leader, then you are a leader for life. In Romans 11, Paul is speaking about Israel and their current blindness to the truth. He states that his covenant with them will not be broken. Again, God does not break his word. In verse 29 he says, *for the gifts and calling of God are without repentance.* Again, what God puts into place, no man, no law, no church member, or religious board member is ever going to change. If God was so emphatic about stating that divorce was not his idea and that he never changes and every other statement about God in his word supports this fact, then why in the world as the church do we allow our fallen leaders to be ostracized, kicked out, trampled on, and demoralized because of a failure? I wish I could scream into the world's largest megaphone and tell the church to *stop!* With this very act, that happens unfortunately every year in our churches, how can we expect people to believe there is recovery for their own mistakes? How can we preach that God is a forgiving God and that he will make all things new when they watch us strip our failed leaders to nothing and all we allow them to do after their failure is pay tithe?

If the failed leader does not repent and will not admit their failure, then the issue is on them. But when we have leaders who admit, repent, and honorably take a seat from leading until they find themselves back in the arms of God, we have an obligation to do what God does: welcome them back home without reservation. Sure, there will be a process to earn back the people's respect, but at least we should help them do so. When the prodigal son came back home, the father did not tell him he could hang out there and sit there, but he would never be considered of value again. No way; he put the family ring (authority) back on him, dressed him with family royal attire (covering), and threw a party. Was there damage to the family for what the prodigal did? Sure there was. The brother was bitter and hated his brother after that horrible ordeal. But, as you see in this story, the father blamed the elder brother for the bitterness, not the prodigal. If you are a pastor and you are reading this and say that you don't agree, then I beg of you never to preach about the prodigal again because you just don't get it!

The devil is laughing at the church's biggest blunder of all time. We preach one thing and do another. So, I ask you: are we to blame for the ever-increasing lack of commitment in our homes, our communities, and our government? We just might be.

Throughout Scripture in the New Testament, the church is referred to as the bride of Christ. This is very exciting to me. If God considers me to be a part of that bride, then I have this assurance: he will never leave me nor forsake me. God does not believe in divorce, and this is great news for the church. But as a failed leader myself, this gives me great comfort. This tells me that though I fail, I can repent, get cleaned up, and try harder than ever to be better today than the day before, and Christ smiles at me as his spotless bride. And from here, God sees me exactly as he called me to be: first as his child, second as a leader. And it is this calling that is without repentance.

If I remember correctly, there is this one story about a leader that I heard about that made a horrible mistake. You know, one of those *big* ones. He was a great leader. In fact, at that time, he would have been considered one of this world's greatest leaders, even according to today's standards. However, he had a moment in his life that led to compromise. There have been many explanations, reasons, excuses, or just stories given by all who know the events of his life. You know, the kind of reasons or explanations that only the "I haven't made that kind of mistake" kind of people tell their friends and congregations. Regardless, he was a man that was considered one of the greatest guys you could meet. But his *big* mistake led to another really bad decision. Often is the case with sin. One sin will lead to another.

Down the road a bit, he was confronted after being found out about his blunder. He was quick to repent and did what he could to make things right. The cost of his sin was high. I mean really high. I mean oxygen mask-needed high. As a result of his sin, the woman he committed the affair with became pregnant. The baby died. Death is hard enough, but when an unwilling child becomes a forced participant in a drama he/she had nothing to do with, that is just too much. Not a good day.

As I said, he did what he could to make it right, but there was nothing that he could do. Thank God for the blood of the Lamb. Only the blood of an innocent man could cause this kind of blunder to be corrected. The greatest part is that he is considered one of the greatest figures of Christendom today. In fact, he is even considered "a man after God's own heart." Yeah, you know him, King David. Not bad for a failed leader, is it? This is probably a stretch, but I say that this has not been said about too many of us today, even if you are as clean as Mr. Clean's bald head.

I had a pastor once tell me in conversation about this very thing that King David was not allowed to build the temple because of his affair with Bathsheba. I started to laugh because I actually knew where he was going, and I have to admit that I set him up for that one. I cannot find in Scripture anywhere that God said he could not build the new temple because he had a fling with Bathsheba. In fact, in 1 Chronicles 28:3, the prophet told David that he could not build the house of God because he was a man of war and had shed blood. Not one thing was ever mentioned because of his affair and subsequent scheme to have Uriah killed in battle. There is another verse of Scripture that is very enlightening on this subject. 1 Samuel 16:18 tells of the story right after the discovery of little David as a shepherd boy and his anointing as the future king. Little David is called to play and sing for King Saul. As the pick for a talented musician is being searched out, little David the shepherd boy was identified as a cunning player, mighty valiant man, and what else, you guessed it, "a man of war." So David was considered by all that knew him, including God, as "a man of war" long before his dream to build a house for God, and also long before his failure. Sorry, but even God himself does not consider failure disqualification from being used by him for his glory.

There is a resounding tone being set here. David's moral failure did not disqualify him, but it does appear that the shedding of blood did. The next time you are out for blood against a preacher or leader who failed, be careful that you don't kill him or shed his blood by demanding he never function as a leader (his God-given calling) again. If you do, you may lose your own place in ministry and may be disqualified to build the house of God any further.

Whether you admit it or not, as a leader you are flawed and have blown it a few times. No one may have noticed it or found out, but you still have sinned just like everyone else. For the record, I do not believe that failed leaders cannot be restored. I have witnessed many failed leaders become some of the most effective and life-changing leaders in America. If only they could tell us their stories without fear of retribution from the one place that should hold them up, the church. If you still believe that failed leaders can no longer lead and cannot be effective in the ministry, then you may want to get out of the ministry yourself. But I have one last thing to say about this: *but from the beginning it hath not been so.*

Chapter 7

He Buys Ugly Houses

Have you ever noticed while studying the four Gospels how Jesus constantly went against the grain of the Pharisees? I am not sure there was a day that went by that Jesus did not in some way challenge the philosophies and rituals of this stubborn folk. He seemed to stay in hot water with these guys and never did they agree on anything. Jesus had a knack for challenging the rituals and beliefs of this animated group of people. I imagine it would have been fun to watch because it sure can be fun to read the stories.

In Luke 15, such a story takes place. There, Jesus does what no one else would do. He associated with sinners, common folk, and this just blew their minds. They immediately start complaining amongst themselves and trying to figure a way to capture Jesus in some sort of law breaking. Now if you will notice, the Scripture never makes mention that he ever acknowledged their murmuring. He just simply starts teaching them by using a parable. Of course, the parable would end up being an indictment against their pious ways of living, but nonetheless, he exposes them.

The parable is depicted with a scene that has a shepherd looking for that one lost lamb. *What man of you, having an hundred sheep, if he lose one of them, doth not leave the ninety and nine in the wilderness, and go after that which is lost, until he find it?* (Luke 15:4). I am sure that the question was met with some resistance entwined with pride; however, it was a valuable question that, even today, the church has a hard time answering when it comes to lost leaders.

He goes on to say in verses 5–7, *And when he hath found it, he layeth it on his shoulders, rejoicing. And when he cometh home, he calleth together his friends and neighbours, saying unto them, Rejoice with me; for I have found my sheep which was lost. I say unto you, that likewise joy shall be in heaven over one sinner that repenteth, more than over ninety and nine just persons, which need no repentance.* This Scripture is so cool and has so much to say about what God feels about even one lost person. God goes after them and looks until he finds them. Oh, thank God for the never ending mercy of his love.

But in our churches and organizations, that's not how it normally turns out. We have this modus oprandi that we use, I believe, unknowingly at times. We base what and who we hang around on the present day value of a person's life. This is not a new thing that we do, either. We are told all our lives to associate with only the best of people. As if we can truly judge that. Scripture teaches that it is nearly impossible to know the heart of a man. Only God himself can do that. You may say that you judge them by their fruits. Okay, I will give you that. But how do you know what fruit they will produce next season? They may have a problem now, and their fruit resembles that currently. But do you know what is going to happen tomorrow?

The fact is that it is impossible for you to view tomorrow right now in the present. We have got to back off of each other a bit and give room for correction because it is impossible for you to know what I will be a year from now. I may be messed up today, but God may swoop in and change everything tomorrow for me. You can't possibly know that.

That is what is so great about God. He does not just view me as I am, but he views me as what he believes I can be. He is not just a God of yesterday and today, but he is a God of tomorrow. He is not just a God that was and is, but he is a God that is to come. He fills all time and space, the past, present, and future. He is not just my author, but he is the finisher of who I will be in him. Clearly, he is the alpha *and* omega. He is not just the beginning, but he is also the ending. You may be viewing me in the middle of my walk with him, but he not only sees where I am right now, he also sees me at the end of my journey. *For I know the thoughts that I think toward you, saith the Lord, thoughts of peace, and not of evil, to give you an expected end* (Jeremiah 29:11). He says that I can depend on something: that he sees an end that will be designed just for me regardless of what I look like now.

There is a real estate company that launched an ad campaign several years ago. They bought up billboards all over the Southeast that had a background of a bright, ugly color of yellow. The tagline they used was "We Buy Ugly Houses." There was hardly an interstate that you drove down that you did not see at least one of those big attention-grabbing signs. They wanted everyone to know that if you had a house that you needed to get rid of, regardless of its condition, they wanted it. They could do this because they understood that regardless of what it looked like before they purchased it, they knew what it would become after they got it in their hands.

We serve a God that understands that life may have taken its toll on us and we failed to live up to our potential. But, God understands that if we can just get back into his hands we will live to our fullest potentials as leaders. Why? Because God buys ugly houses. He has an investment plan that will restore you to your former glory and then some. He knows your worth and has already paid your price.

Back to Luke 15. The Pharisees and the scribes noticed that Jesus gathered with the sinners and publicans. The word *sinners* here in the Greek is *hamartolos* (ham-ar-to-los'); one who misses the mark.

It means they looked at them as worthless or of no value. Jesus then asked them the question in verse 4: How many of you that have one hundred sheep and had lost one of them would leave the 99 and go find the one? We say amen to this and we all may get excited about it, but let me ask you the question in a way that hits home. How many of you who have a hundred one dollar bills and were to lose one would go out and find the one? Not many of us would. Why? Because we think in terms of "oh well, I have the majority and that is good enough."

If you have ever put a puzzle together and lost just one piece, it messes with the whole thing and will never be complete. You may be able to identify what the picture is, but that missing piece will always be a problem, and therefore the puzzle will never be complete. God views you in the same way. He will not ever be satisfied until you come back home and return to the place that he designed for you as a leader.

The fact is that when we sin, it does take its toll on us. We lose out and lose big. But God took care of the price of sin a long time ago. I never find in Scripture where he ever put in the parameters of whether or not you were in leadership. He gave his life for all. *For unto us a child is born, unto us a son is given: and the government shall be upon his shoulder: and his name shall be called Wonderful, Counsellor, The mighty God, The everlasting Father, The Prince of Peace* (Isaiah 9:6). Notice the statement "the government shall be upon his shoulders." Did you also notice that when he found the lost lamb that he puts the lamb in the exact same place the government was placed? Could it be that he is trying to tell us that though the law of sin does apply because you failed, that now he has taken on that law and now he will judge you in his court? You now can sit in his law chamber and his law says that you can be and will be restored if you allow him. Sure, you may have walked out on God and failed as a leader, but God is willing to restore your ugly house.

I want to close this chapter with another Scripture reference that shows how God expects his chosen to act when it comes to failure.

Therefore thus saith the Lord God; An adversary there shall be even round about the land; and he shall bring down thy strength from thee, and thy palaces shall be spoiled. Thus saith the Lord; As the shepherd taketh out of the mouth of the lion two legs, or a piece of an ear; so shall the children of Israel be taken out that dwell in Samaria in the corner of a bed, and in Damascus in a couch (Amos 3:11–12).

Amos says to Israel that there is an adversary that roams their land. Today there seems to be an assault on leadership like never before. Never has the integrity of leadership been more challenged than in our lifetime. I beg of you, if you have been able to maintain your integrity thus far, please know your limits and your boundaries as leaders. Sorry, just felt like I needed to add that. I move on.

He says that there is a shepherd that comes up on the scene of a lamb that obviously messed up and fell into the grasp of the adversary. The lamb is already captured before the shepherd could get there. The scene is gruesome and grotesque at best. The lamb is worthless and is inside the adversary's mouth. The lamb now has no identity because its face is gone. Its head is missing. It can't think of a way to get itself out of the mess. All that is left is two legs and a piece of an ear. Why in the world would the shepherd continue to save the lamb? Because that is what God did for a lost and messed up world. He surveyed the scene and it looked bad, really bad, and little hope existed for men and women to survive. Yet, he stepped in and recovered what seemed non-recoverable.

There may be only a semblance of what once was a leader after they have failed. But we have a scriptural mandate to recover what we can. It may be only two legs and just a piece of an ear, but God worked with much less when he originally created us. He only had his word.

I have just got to add this last thing before I bring this chapter to its end. If I told you that there was a one hundred dollar bill hidden within the pages of this book, would you look for it? There is not one of you that would not, and in fact, most of you just left this chapter looking for it. Okay, now that you are back, let me add something here. There is a problem. This one hundred dollar bill was found in the dirt and stepped on many times. Do you still want it? Oh, this one hundred dollar bill has also been crushed and wrinkled badly. Do you still want it? Hold on a minute, there is more. I also noticed that this one hundred dollar bill was picked up by a dog, chewed on, and eventually spit out, leaving it soaked with saliva. Do you still want it? Do you really? Why? I think I know why and let me take a crack at it here.

Even though this one hundred dollar bill has been lost, stepped on, crushed, wrinkled, chewed up, and spit out, you still want it because you understand the value of a one hundred dollar bill. So, even though that failed leader may have been stepped on, crushed, wrinkled, chewed up, and spit out, God still wants him. Why? Because God understands his value!

As I travel this country back and forth and visit the numerous churches across this land, I am seeing more and more run-down, shattered shells of leadership. Leadership that once had it all together and looked great, functioned well, and gave their communities definition, but now are vacated structures of what once was. They are just sitting there with nothing going on inside. The electricity that once powered them has now been cut off. They have lost connection with their source of life. However, I want you to know that there is a new investor in town, and he is buying up everything. He is anticipating the next surge in the market and knows that if he can just get his hands on them long enough, he can transform them into lively, productive structures for his purpose once again. Why? Because He loves to buy ugly houses. This man has a knack for restoration.

Chapter 8

Innocent for Lack of Evidence

Have you ever been accused of anything where you know they had you dead to rights? You know, that kind of situation where it is absolutely impossible for you to get out of the trouble that is soon to follow a really bad mistake? As kids I am sure we were all there most days. At least for me, it seemed for several years that I just could not avoid it. Then that big one would happen and I just knew there was no way to get out of it.

I remember being at home one evening and it seems there was something I wanted to do or somewhere I wanted to go, but my parents refused. I remember being so enraged as I walked back into my bedroom, just fuming over the fact that they said no. I paced my bedroom floor back and forth from one side to the other, just venting under my breath words that I dare not write in this book. Needless to say, there was much repenting needed after things cooled down. But before I could get my composure, I lay down on my bed, seething, and rolled over and kicked the wall, creating a Grand Canyon of a hole. Just as the moment my foot went through the wall, I knew I was totally in for it. Oh, the feeling that came over me that I had blown it and blown it really big. At that time, I wore a size seven and a half shoe, and my foot went halfway into that wall.

I can still feel that cold feeling that swept over me and ran down me from the top of my head to the bottom of my half-inserted foot. I knew I was in for it! As I removed my foot, the sickening feeling became worse as the damage became more evident. Oh yes, there was a hole, and a twelve-year-old would not be able to fix this one. I panicked! I ran around my room looking for ways to cover it up. I used pillows. I rearranged furniture and tried every possible way to get that hole fixed. I remember my mother coming to the door and wanting to know what was going on. I covered the hole up again with pillows and it saved me for a small amount of time. She left not knowing what had happened, but I knew my time on earth was short.

After several minutes of trying to find ways to cover it up, I knew that it was over for me. There was just no possible way to fix this issue without going to someone that knew how to fix holes. Unfortunately, my dad was the only one in the house that could do it. Yet, he was the only one I was trying to avoid. Ouch! I can still remember the pain when the verdict that was issued in my head stated that I would have to tell him. However, I tried one last thing. I came up with this story that I was just playing around and knocked the picture off the wall, and it made the hole with the corner of the frame. Pretty good, I thought. Judge me if you will, but I bet you have made some pretty lousy defenses yourself growing up and probably still do.

As I told the story to my dad, he just gave me that look. All the evidence pointed to the facts. The hole even looked like a shoe print, and the picture frame had no evidence of such a fall. My dad's face said it all: "Son, I know what happened and there is no way out of it." For a moment, he paused, and then just like that, he stopped trying to convince me of my false testimony and came back later to fix the wall. Within minutes he fixed the hole and made it as if nothing had ever happened. Both of us knew what happened and both of us were waiting on the other to make the next move. Well, I could not stand it any longer, so I broke. I told him what happened and recanted my story. However, for both of us, there was something that had taken place. The hole was no longer there. Neither was there any evidence of a hole or that something unfortunate had taken place. I will never forget what my dad did for me that day. He knew the evidence, yet he covered it up and made it as if it had never happened. I was "innocent for lack of evidence."

The first ten verses of John 18 tell a story that has become very famous in its own right. Jesus and the disciples are in the garden just prior to Jesus' arrest and trial. They have been there praying for what seemed an eternity to the chosen twelve (minus one, of course). The rustling of a large crowd with the faint hints of swords clanging against bushes and rocks approached in the distance. The flickering of dim lanterns could now be seen. As they entered the area, a familiar face could be seen by the disciples. It's Judas. Can you imagine the thoughts that ran through Peter's head when he recognized Judas? Peter knew in his heart what was about to take place. He knew what Jesus had said about this moment and was going to try and avoid it at all cost.

When Jesus made it clear who he was to everyone there, Peter could not stand it any longer. He whips out a sword and lunges for the first person he can reach. Poor Malchus! He was closer than anyone and unarmed, but he still paid a price. Peter, with one fell swoop, cuts off this man's ear. Now we know where Mike Tyson gets it. He was just being biblical. I know it is a bit of a stretch, but it could've worked had he been smart enough to use that argument.

According to the book of John, chapter 18, this pretty much ends this story. Nothing more is said from this viewpoint. So as did John, I am going to leave you here and take you back to an earlier event that is just as cruel as this one. In the first ten verses of John 8, there is a story that has its own roots in cruelty. We all know the story well. It was the woman caught in the bed of adultery. Notice how they only brought the women? The Jews in that day had a really corrupt way of enforcing morality.

The story of this woman is a sordid one at best. As I already stated, it shows the corruptness of man when left to his own righteousness, and yet it ends in beauty rarely seen when it concerns the Pharisees. There are several characters acting out this drama. I want you to imagine the harshness of their faces and the anger in their voices as it rang out across the streets of their ancient town. We have no indication what led this woman or the missing man into such a stormy event of emotions. We do not know what caused this woman to act as she did to satisfy the pleasures of this man. I am sure there is much more that could have been useful to us, but God decided we did not need to know the specifics. Suffice it to say, she was caught dead to rights.

From all indications, she was approaching the end of her life due to her committed act of sin. It was all over for her—finished, convicted, and death lying at the door. It is one thing to be guilty of sin, but to be caught in the act of sin takes on a whole different feel and just makes it that much more degrading.

So here we have this drama unfolding in the eyes of all present. All that knew her knew her sin. It was all out in the open, thanks to those that felt they were superior. The story gives indication that the Pharisees had practiced for this kind of thing. They knew exactly how to get what they wanted, the death of a failed person. The faces of the Pharisees were set in stone and displayed the guilty verdict to all there that day. The witnesses stared at her with contempt, knowing what was about to take place. She is thrown at the feet of Jesus like yesterday's trash in the dirty streets. I must mention here that there was a twofold purpose for throwing her into the public view. First, they knew in their hearts just what kind of man Jesus was and what he most likely felt about the situation. Another matter for another book later, maybe, but they also wanted his head. Secondly, if the public opinion could be swayed, their desired guilty verdict was a sure thing.

There she lay at the feet of Jesus, embarrassed, ashamed, wounded, and bruised from the Pharisees abuse. Her case is opened and set in motion. When they brought the charges to the open forum, they used law to back them up. Sure, the law does apply here, but there is something they are forgetting. Jesus begins to write in the same dirt this woman lies in. "He who is without sin cast the first stone." This line of reasoning had never been brought into the court of law before. Now, their grip on the stones they had already picked up and readied to throw lessened somewhat. They pondered the statement. Jesus writes again on the ground. Then all of a sudden, one by one, from the oldest to the youngest, they dropped their stones and walked away.

For the first time, Jesus and the accused are left alone. Jesus speaks and asks a question. "Where are your accusers?" The witnesses, the angry faces, and any evidence that was to be presented were now running back into hiding with the Pharisees. She answers Jesus and tells him that "no one is here." Because the witnesses and the evidence they carried are now gone, she is "innocent for lack of evidence." Jesus speaks again and says, "Neither do I accuse you so go and sin no more." Jesus did not give a big lecture or run her finger in a pencil sharpener or humiliate her. He simply says you're innocent and don't do this again. No twelve steps to recovery for failed leaders. None of this "you have to earn your way back" type of stuff. Just go and do your best not to mess up again. It doesn't sit well with you, does it? Everyone reading this is begging to see if there were more requirements, but there were not. Jesus is really weird that way. He steps in, covers the sin, and renews the offender. I think that is what the whole cross thing was about. Just guessing.

Earlier, I left you with Peter in the book of John 18, whacking off the ear of Malchus, the servant to the high priest. But before we go there, things only get worse for Peter. He ends up denying Christ three times. He backslides and returns to his old lifestyle of fishing. Later, after the crucifixion, Jesus appears on the seashore and Peter catches a glimpse of him. Peter has one of those "come to Jesus meetings" and Jesus asks Peter some of the most famous questions ever quoted in the Bible. "Do you love me?" Not once, but three times. One for every denial, I guess.

I have a question for you. Do you ever find where Peter ever paid the price for whacking off the ear of Malchus? Do you ever find where he spent time in jail? This was a heinous and cruel act. Malchus was left with a horrible-looking injury according to John. However, if you study a bit further, the physician Luke records the rest of the story. Luke 22 verse 51 says that Jesus picked up the ear and healed him. The fact that he was healed does not negate the fact that Peter committed the crime. But where there is no evidence to present, the law of innocence prevails.

In Knights Master Book of 4,000 Illustrations the story is told of a man walking on the seashore in the Valley of Dead Men at the South Sea Islands. He looked back at his path and, in spite of his best efforts, it was crooked and twisted. He became exhausted and weary trying so hard to walk straight but to no avail. He fell asleep and was awakened several hours later. He thought to himself, I will never be able to walk straight. He thought he would glance back at his twisted, crooked path and he was startled at what he saw. You see, during his sleep, the tide came in and washed away every crooked step he made. Suddenly he realized and was assured by God that for every path you take that turns out crooked, he has a tide that will wash away your twisted, crooked paths. He was no longer a man with a crooked walking past; he was "innocent for lack of evidence."

Chapter 9

Shameful Kinfolk

E very one of us has both kinfolk that we are proud of and that we are ashamed of. I think every family has that cousin that, well, let's just say, had they done things a bit differently in their lives, we would be able to hold our heads a little higher in public. Never is this more evident than at the annual family reunion. Everything is clicking along and then Cousin Billy shows up. Or maybe it's Aunt Mabel. You know, the one that has been married a half dozen times and everyone knows the guy she is with won't last past Thanksgiving.

As they pull up to the reunion, a quick historical recital is given to all those there in a hurried fashion before they get too close. When they step out of the car, everyone cringes and braces for that ear-piercing, "I am here." Now the party can begin, they claim. I think God gets a kick out of keeping families humble by introducing those specimens of bad seed into the family tree.

The genealogy of Christ is a fascinating one to say the least. It is chock-full of a list of names, some popular, and some not so popular. I have this poster-sized listing of the family tree of Christ in my office at home. As you are looking at it, you get a sense of historic importance of these chronicled names. Each tells their own story. Again, some stories are more popular than others. Some came and went without so much as a ripple in the waters of history as it was written. There are those on there that seemed to be great and wonderful people, living life as giving, peaceful, and accommodating folk, never stepping out of line or swaying one way or the other from what is right and wrong. Just good-hearted people living life. Then there are those that just bring shame to the family. You know the kind. And yes, even in Jesus' family tree, there are some real characters. Let's take a look at Matthew 1.

Matthew 1:1–16

The book of the generation of Jesus Christ, the son of David, the son of Abraham. Abraham begat Isaac; and Isaac begat Jacob; and Jacob begat Judah and his brethren; and Judah begat Perez and Zerah of Tamar; and Perez begat Hezron; and Hezron begat Ram; and Ram begat Amminadab; and Amminadab begat Nahshon; and Nahshon begat Salmon; and Salmon begat Boaz of Rahab; and Boaz begat Obed of Ruth; and Obed begat Jesse; and Jesse begat David the king. And David begat Solomon of her that had been the wife of Uriah; and Solomon begat Rehoboam; and Rehoboam begat Abijah; and Abijah begat Asa; and Asa begat Jehoshaphat; and Jehoshaphat begat Joram; and Joram begat Uzziah; and Uzziah begat Jotham; and Jotham begat Ahaz; and Ahaz begat Hezekiah; and Hezekiah begat Manasseh; and Manasseh begat Amon; and Amon begat Josiah; and Josiah begat Jechoniah and his brethren, at the time of the carrying away to Babylon. And after the carrying away to Babylon, Jechoniah begat Shealtiel; and Shealtiel begat Zerubbabel; and Zerubbabel begat Abiud; and Abiud begat Eliakim; and Eliakim begat Azor; and Azor begat Sadoc; and Sadoc begat Achim; and Achim begat Eliud; and Eliud begat Eleazar; and Eleazar begat Matthan; and Matthan begat Jacob; and

Jacob begat Joseph the husband of Mary, of whom was born Jesus, who is called Christ.

Try saying that list of names twice in the same day. It makes my head hurt just thinking about it. As monotonous and pointless as it may seem to list the names out, there is real significance entwined within. From the very start, God decided to bring to the forefront two different names; David and Abraham. We all know that Abraham was the first dude that God decided to create himself a nation with. And we also know that David was promised that his seed would forever remain on the throne. But if you look at them more closely, you will find these two guys were not without failure. We will show that next. Let's start with the first one listed and work our way to Jesus. Of course, this list of names only shows the male side of the tree. There are a few interesting female characters that I will speak of later.

Abraham–disobeyed God by bringing Lot and his family along and doubted that God would make him a nation.

Isaac–good dude.

Jacob–a deceiver and liar.

Judah–hired a prostitute and sold his brother to Egypt. He was also a liar.

Phares–no significance

Zara–no significance

Esrom–no significance

Aram–no significance

Aminadab–no significance

Naasson–no significance

Salmon–no significance

Boaz–good dude.

Obed–the son of Ruth, the Moabite. Half-breed.

Jesse–good dude and father of David.

David–man after God's own heart; liar, adulterer, and murderer.

Solomon–the wisest man ever to live. Married over one thousand women and served idols. Mother was Bathsheba.

Roboam–no significance

Abia–no significance

Asa–no significance

Jehoshaphat–good dude.

Joram–good dude.

Ozias–no significance

Jotham–no significance

Achaz–no significance

Ezekias–no significance

Manasses–no significance

Amon–no significance

Josiah–good dude.

Jechoniah–no significance

Shealtiel–no significance

Zerubbabel–good dude.

Abiud–no significance

Eliakim–no significance

Azor–no significance

Sadoc–no significance

Achim–no significance

Eliud–no significance

Eleazar–no significance

Matthan–no significance

Jacob–no significance

Joseph–good dude.

Okay, thank God that is over. My hands are starting to cramp. As you can see, there are several people listed that just live life, and for the most part, are unheard of without much drama. However, it is the most notable ones that seem to get all the attention. Bad attention at times, I might add. There are at least six members of this family that had some real issues. Never would have thought that the family of Jesus would have had so many issues, would you? But it is true.

This should give you hope. Even though they were the line of Jesus, and as flawed as they were, Jesus still chose them to be his lineage. Think about Judah. You know "praise" don't you? The one we always look to for direction in worship and praise services, oh yeah, he was a real character. Hired a prostitute, lied to her, and prior to that, sold his brother Joseph down the river. They even named a nation after him, and we have this neat little phrase we use: "Lion of Judah." Pretty cool, isn't it?

Think about King David. A dysfunctional father best describes this dude. Cheater, liar, and murderer go well with his name. His son hated him and he allowed his daughter to be raped. David was such a lustful man that to make sure he was dead, they made a young virgin lay on top of him to see what he would do. Yet, he is known as a man after God's own heart. What gives? I will tell you what gives. God knew the entire time that man was messed up from the garden and he had a plan to redeem every single one of them, if only they would let him. His plan was to come to this earth and cover all sin with his blood once and for all. Where did this doctrine of "once a failure, always a failure" come from? It came from the pits of hell, I tell you. That's my story and I am sticking to it.

What about some of the females of this lineage? Rahab was a harlot and prostitute who hid the Israelites and married into the family. Ruth was a Moabite (a heathen nation), who also married into the family. And Tamar played as a harlot and tricked Judah. All of these women were responsible for producing the offspring that became the lineage of Christ.

The next time you get on your high horse about how leadership and ministry must remain without reproach (and that is true and we should strive to it), just remember that even Jesus had some "shameful kinfolk" in his family and yet he wasn't afraid to name them as kinfolk.

The Process of Restoration

Chapter 10

The Elephant in the Room

I t has happened in every church, synagogue, mosque, and place of worship in the world. And it will happen again. In fact, it is probably happening right now, right under your nose. The best and meticulously planned effort will not keep it from happening. If it has happened once, it will happen again and again and again. As long as there are people in positions of leadership and ministry, failure will continue to show up and take its seat on the front row of your place of worship.

I am sure you can point to countless times you have witnessed this happen, and not just in someone else's church. You were there and you witnessed the whole thing. You noticed something was wrong with that leader, but you could not quite put your finger on it. He had changed and become irritable and moody. He did not seem to have the same drive as before. He missed more and more church events and just had a feel of secrecy about them not ever noticed before. The leader had become more and more distant, with stress becoming his closest friend. Yet you said nothing.

Then it happens. The telltale signs of a major failure have come to fruition. Maybe he was found out. Maybe he was noble enough to confess and resign before it became public. Every situation is different. Regardless, the shock is almost unbearable. The congregation stumbles under the weight of the news. Disbelief is tantamount to the pain experienced as you watch your beloved leader disappear under the mounds of harsh words and criticism. The words spoken by unloving members only add to the atmosphere of distrust and the rumor mill. And there he sits. That elephant in the room that no one knows exactly what to do with.

He will sit there for years and never say a word, only to sound off every time a leader fails. If your church is lucky, you will only experience this a few times. If you are unlucky, it may be your senior pastor that falls. But either way, the elephant will become a member of your church. The problem is that you will become used to him sitting there. You will get used to looking around him, over him, or through him if you must, but just the same, you will forget he is there until the next time. Each time calls for the same action as before, but no one does anything. Everyone simply sits by as another leader falls by the wayside and is discarded like yesterday's trash.

It is beyond me how the church that claims to have the answers to life's drama and many twists and turns freezes up when it comes to failed leaders. Or worse yet, we dump them in the wasteland of "once was." Whether they are a Sunday school teacher who goes through a divorce or the music director of a large church that has an affair, the result is the same. The elephant moves into our organizations.

This elephant is that big massive question *why?* Why do we do what we do when leaders fall? Why we are not better prepared for the failing leader is beyond me. How many talented leaders have we lost because we just did not know what to do with them? I would dare say thousands. We can chose to ignore this massive problem or someone, somewhere, can stand up and be a true leader and give the church direction with this issue. For the record, if I haven't already stated it, I am no way implying that the failed leader not be held accountable for his/her actions. I am saying exactly the opposite. Letting failed leaders walk out the door and not restoring them is not holding them accountable. It is kicking them out and not doing what Christ called the church to do—"to seek and save that which is lost." Meanwhile, leaders walk away from the church and fall deeper into sin because they have nowhere to turn. Tell me how that fits into what Jesus has called the church to do.

As I said, every church has most likely experienced this kind of thing within its ranks. Until you figure out what is best for you and your church, it will continue to happen. Some seem to think that a restoration policy in your church will give license to others to sin at will. I completely disagree with that and feel that it is a copout. The process of restoration is something that I promise no one that has failed wants to go through. It will require that the leader face his failure every time the church doors are open. It will also require that the church learn how to love unconditionally even though they are also hurt. It is a process that will take time and energy and may even cause some to leave and seek other places of membership. You cannot fear that if it happens. If they leave, they do not have the heart of Christ and therefore are wayward in their walk with him, and they themselves will need restoring.

Every failure has its own set of circumstances and situations. Each leader is different and will respond in a unique way to how things come down. There will be some that will wait until they are exposed. There are some that will buckle under the weight of sin and confess to their pastor. Each situation must be handled uniquely and carefully. I attended a Catalyst one-day conference where that very question on how to handle failed leaders was presented to Craig Groschell. Craig stated it in a way that I thought was incredibly unique and refreshing. He stated that when a leader falls in his church, there are levels of grace that he uses. If a leader comes and admits it without being questioned about it, then there is a lot of grace factored in. If a leader is found out, and then admits it, a little less grace is factored in. If a leader has failed and it is found that it is lifestyle with him/her and it is something that has been ongoing for a lengthy period, even less grace is factored in. He stated that if a leader has been found out and will not repent and refuses to make the necessary changes, then that situation is approached with even less grace than the other previously mentioned examples.

There are also things to think about such as "exposure." If the situation is not exposed to the general public, then nothing needs to be brought out before the people if it can be handled behind closed doors. However, some situations are out in the public view long before even the head leadership is notified that there is a problem. In these cases, they must be dealt with before the people, but even then, in limited measure. Details should never be brought before the congregation. You are only asking for trouble if you do that. Besides, that is justifying gossip. You will create more issues by telling the details and you will also stir up more things than you ever dreamed of. There is no scriptural support for public humiliation concerning a leader's failure. Jesus never did it, and neither should we.

I want to address a Scripture that was used by a minister to give support for the action of publicly addressing a fallen leader's sin. This minister went so far as to say that the humiliation would keep the fallen leader from failing again. 1 Timothy 5:19 is where we pick up. The letter to Timothy is written from Paul and these verses in particular are dealing with how he should handle elders (leaders). *Against an elder receive not an accusation, but by two or three witnesses.* Seems pretty straightforward, but how many times have we heard gossip and accused the leader as if it was already a known fact to have taken place? We need to tread lightly concerning these things.

I want to quote *Matthew Henry's Commentary* on the matter, perhaps to shed a bit more light:

> Concerning the accusation of ministers (1Ti 5:19): Against an elder receive not an accusation, but before two or three witnesses. Here is the Scripture-method of proceeding against an elder, when accused of any crime. Observe, 1. There must

be an accusation; it must not be a flying uncertain report, but an accusation, containing a certain charge, must be drawn up. Further, He is not to be proceeded against by way of enquiry; this is according to the modern practice of the inquisition, which draws up articles for men to purge themselves of such crimes, or else to accuse themselves; but, according to the advice of Paul, there must be an accusation brought against an elder. 2. This accusation is not to be received unless supported by two or three credible witnesses; and the accusation must be received before them, that is, the accused must have the accusers face to face, because the reputation of a minister is, in a particular manner, a tender thing; and therefore, before anything be done in the least to blemish that reputation, great care should be taken that the thing alleged against him be well proved, that he be not reproached upon an uncertain surmise;

Matthew Henry's Commentary is precise with accepting the accusation. All top leaders of churches and organizations would do well to follow this method outlined in verse 19. However, verse 20 talks about the publicity of the matter, should it go there. *Them that sin rebuke before all, that others also may fear.* This is the verse I mentioned that the minister I was discussing this with said was the prescription to handling an individual's sin. Of course I disagreed with him and this is why. I again will quote *Matthew Henry's Commentary* and will also add a quote from Albert *Barnes' Notes on the Bible.*

"but (1Ti-5:20) those that sin rebuke before all; that is, thou needest not be so tender of other people, but rebuke them publicly." Or "those that sin before all rebuke before all, that the plaster may be as wide as the wound, and that those who are in danger of sinning by the example of their fall may take warning by the rebuke given them for it, that others also may fear." Observe, (1.) Public scandalous sinners must be rebuked publicly: as their sin has been public, and committed before many, or at least come to the hearing of all, so their reproof must be public, and before all. (2.) Public rebuke is designed for the good of others, that they may fear, as well as for the good of the party rebuked; hence it was ordered under the law that public offenders should receive public punishment, that all Israel might hear, and fear, and do no more wickedly.

Barnes' Notes:

1 Tim 5:20: Them that sin - That have been proved to have committed sin - referring probably to the elders mentioned in the previous verse, but giving the direction so general a form that it might be applicable to others.

Rebuke before all - Before all the church or congregation. The word "rebuke" properly denotes to reprove or reprehend. It means here that there should be a public statement of the nature of the offence, and such a censure as the case demanded. It extends only to spiritual censures. There is no power given of inflicting any punishment by fine or imprisonment. The power of the church, in such cases, is only to express its strong and decided disapprobation of the wrong done, and, if the case demands it, of disowning the offending member or minister. This direction to "rebuke an offender before all," may be easily reconciled with the direction in 1Ti 5:1, "Rebuke not an elder." The latter refers to the private and pastoral conversation with an elder, and to the method in which he should be treated in such contact - to wit, with the feelings due to a father; the direction here refers to the manner in which an offender should be treated who has been proved to be guilty, and where the case has become public. Then there is to be a public expression of disapprobation.

That others also may fear - That they may be kept from committing the same offence; compare 1Pe 2:14. The end of punishment is not the gratification of the private feelings of him who administers it, but the prevention of crime.

As leaders, pastors, bishops, etc., we deal daily with those we are responsible for and the unique situations that encompass their lives. Not ever are we supposed to divulge this information to anyone unless directed by the individual. Why, then, do we feel the need to divulge this same type of information to our congregations when it comes to leaders? It just makes no sense at all. According to *Barnes' Notes*, 1 Timothy 5:1 may very well warn against that type of information being disseminated. Again, please walk ever so carefully. King David would not put his hand to the corrupt and wayward Saul because he still recognized him as God's anointed. Should we behave any less? I think not.

There is much indication through these verses and the commentaries that we should deal with the unique situations of failed leaders with respect, honor, and privacy. In the event that the problem becomes public, then it is a no-brainer what needs to happen. If there is a leader whose failure becomes public and they do not want to repent or acknowledge their wrongs, then a stern public rebuke of that sin should be addressed. If we are teaching and preaching correctly to our congregations and organizations, they will, in general, know our feelings against such matters of sin, and it will take limited intervention to set the record straight.

As for the church in these hard situations, they must be taught to respond correctly. Otherwise, they will only ransack and devour the wounded leader. It is a normal response to pain and will happen almost involuntarily. The church will do its best to make decisions in a heightened emotional state, which almost always will end in disaster. Boards will come together and make emotionally-charged statements, stances, and decisions that will be regretted later. All of this and more will happen if the head leadership does not teach and prepare their church or organization to be restoration ready.

A church that can properly handle the restoration of leaders does not happen overnight. It is a long and grueling process. If we are honest, many churches are primarily made up of transplants from other congregations and pastorates. Because we all have our own opinion as to what the Scriptures teach us about failed leaders, the message can seem to be very confusing to those that follow our lead. We are no longer in Kansas, Toto, and failed leaders are everywhere. Be that as it may, it is a sign of the times. We prepare our churches for the latest and greatest moves of society and ready ourselves to be relevant to our communities. Why then are we not ready to restore leaders that have fallen?

A few years ago, on our way to the Atlanta airport, I spoke with Reverend Kenneth Haney for about two hours concerning failed leaders. If you do not know, Bishop Haney was the general superintendent of the United Pentecostal Church International located in St. Louis, Missouri. As I discussed this project with him, he stated with great urgency that we need to be prepared to handle the failed leaders of not only the U.P.C.I., but all organizations worldwide. He shared with me the number of failed leaders he has hosted over the years at his church in Stockton, California. District officials, Sunday school teachers, music directors, musicians, and all facets of leadership have been restored and put back into full-time leadership at his local church. There was a statement he made that just penetrated my heart concerning these restored leaders. He said these same failed but now restored leaders are the very ones who turned his Christian Life Center upside down and are responsible for the success that it is today.

So I ask you, what are you going to do with that elephant in the room? Will you continue to look around it, over it, and possibly through it? Or will you kick it out and replace it with several failed leaders in its place? You never know, that next leader you restore may very well turn your church upside down.

Chapter 11

There is No Place Like Home

The *Wizard of Oz* movie is probably one of the greatest movies of all time. I will never forget the family nights that were centered on the TV, waiting for that airing. It starts off in what appears to be the mundane of black and white and moves quickly into the new era of color. An incredible amount of symbolism is there that we can use, but I will focus in on only a few.

The main character is Dorothy Gale, who lives with her Aunt Em and Uncle Henry in Kansas. She has a loving home and loving relatives. She also has a prized dog that she loves very much. However, there is a problem. There is an old lady (witch) that has it in for the dog. She claims that the dog had bitten her and she has come to lay claim and have it destroyed. This obviously puts Dorothy in a whirlwind of emotions as she begins to plea for the redemption of her prized pup. The family, however, can only shake their heads and tell her that she has to give up her canine. Dorothy will have nothing of it. She plans to run away.

Dorothy leaves home and all that she has ever known because she is not going to lose that dog. However, as she is making her way down the road, a storm that she never anticipated is heading right for her and the home she left behind. In the distance, a funnel cloud can be seen. It is tearing up everything in sight. Dorothy has a momentary clarity of thought and says, "I got to get back home." She starts back, but it's not easy. When she arrives, the family has already gone underground to ride out the storm. What she does not know is that they searched and called for her up until the last moments, but they could not wait any longer.

Dorothy, unable to find her family or get into the storm cellar, dashes into the house and runs into her room, a familiar place of comfort. The house is suddenly and violently struck by the tornado and lifted off its foundation. It begins to spin and cartwheel ever more quickly as it rises above the earth. Dorothy is inside clutching her dog. As it is with every storm, debris is flying everywhere, and eventually, the window comes loose, strikes her head, and leaves her unconscious.

Dorothy awakens, and in short order realizes she is no longer in the black and white world of Kansas and is now living in full color. Sights and sounds that she has never experienced before are all around her. What she notices quickly is that she has killed a wicked witch because her house has fallen on top of her. For a moment, there are celebrations and commendations, and the people of that strange new place are exuberant with gladness. She is a hero to her new land. But then something from her past appears out of nowhere, from the same piece of sky she dropped out of. Yep, the same old lady (witch) has followed her even to the new world of Technicolor.

From this point on, the intention to leave home has changed to getting back home. Her entire journey is now focused on getting back to Kansas. She is instructed by Glinda, the good witch (if there is such a thing), to follow a yellow brick road to see the great and powerful Oz, kind of a type and shadow to God, I guess. As she travels, she encounters several very interesting characters. First, she comes across the Scarecrow, secondly, the Tin Man, and thirdly, a cowardly Lion, all of whom are hoping to receive what they lack (a brain, a heart, and courage, respectively). All of this is done while trying to avoid the wicked witch and her attempt to get her sister's (who Dorothy inadvertently killed) ruby red slippers that Glinda the good witch gave to Dorothy. Why would the good witch give her something that was wanted and desired so badly by her arch enemy? We will try and answer that later.

So Dorothy and her three wary friends make their way to the Emerald City where the great Oz lives. Finally, they will get what they've come for. Not so fast! They are met with resistance, even from the great Oz, who disguises himself as others within his kingdom to test their resolve in getting what they most desire. He puts them through a series of questions and activities before he finally relents. However, before he can give to Dorothy what she truly wants, there is a malfunction with the hot air balloon and the great Oz floats away, out of their reach. Kind of like living for God sometimes, isn't it? Just before we reach that thing or place we need from him, it seems he mysteriously floats away, out of reach.

Shortly thereafter, Dorothy is kidnapped by the wicked witch so she can get her sister's shoes from her. But there is a problem. The shoes can't come off. As long as Dorothy is living, they belong to her. Eventually, Dorothy is rescued by her friends and Glinda blesses them by pointing out that they have always had, right there with them, what they have always wanted. Now it's Dorothy's turn. The whole time, all she had to do was use the shoes. With the click of her heels three times, she is back home and in the safety of her family. She awakens back in the black and white world of Kansas with her family. She tries to tell them all the things that happened and how the whole adventure led her back home. The fact is that this whole thing was a dream, but a dream nonetheless to learn and glean from.

Back to the clicking of the heels thing. As she clicked the heels of her shoes, she makes a statement that "there is no place like home." I have to ask you, is there? Can you think of a place better than home?

I can't. Whenever I think of home, I think of friends and family and the warmth of their love, in spite of what they know about me. And that is the way it is supposed to be. At home there is safety and love no matter what the situation and no matter what the issue. At home you can rest, be fed, and be nurtured. That's why home is so important. If you have a good home, you have everything. You may never make a million dollars or travel the world abroad or see the seven wonders of this world, but if you have a great home, you have all the wonder in the world you will ever need. Our world is screaming for a great home, and few are they who find it.

But why is it when someone messes up or blows it badly they often find themselves leaving home? It has become common practice that when a leader or preacher falls into sin, they are immediately expected to ship out and leave home. I believe this was initially practiced in the interest to protect the fallen, but it actually harms them in the long run. They will be sent to a place that does not know them and cannot adequately care for them, thus the issue that caused the failure cannot be ministered to. This has become such a part of Christian culture today. If you fail, we will just ship you out to a place that does not know your sin; that way you can continue in ministry and leadership and can recover quietly with little or no harm to the church. This has got to be the most backward and incorrect way of handling failed leaders.

Dorothy thought the same thing, and she left town only to get caught up in a much bigger storm. It cost her more than just dealing with the issue at home would have. She was injured and taken to a foreign land, where her troubles only increased. From that point forward, if you remember, all she wanted to do was get home. When a person fails, leaving home is not always the default answer. There are many things to consider in the process. Now, if you are in a church that believes in the death penalty for failed leadership and will not embrace restoration completely, then leaving may be the best choice. That new place will quickly become home because of the spirit of the people there and the heart of their pastor for restoration.

If you are the failed senior pastor of a church and it becomes public, things are different in that situation. As the top leader of that organization, you can't stay there. It will hurt many and drive them away if you do. You will have to find a place that you can go to be healed and be ministered to until you are restored. However, once you are restored, I believe you must return home and give your testimony to those that you hurt and request their forgiveness. You may never actually live there again, but they will know and see your restoration as it lives out in your life.

I urge all pastors and leaders to seriously seek the face of God on this issue. As the symbol of Christ to your congregants and those you lead, you must restore them that have fallen. That is what the ministry of Christ is all about. If you can't fulfill that, then you have failed to be Christlike. When a pastor applies true restoration to his ministering, he gives the fallen leader a second chance, as Christ has given everyone, and he also allows his church to participate in the ultimate calling: restoration. When a fallen leader stays home, it allows the church to participate uniquely in that leader's restoration. They become vested in that leader's spiritual renewal. When they become vested, they become united, and they become partners in His service.

In my failure several years ago, some of the board of directors and ministry board of my church wanted me gone. Understand, I had even repented of what I did and was trying to make things right, but still the hurt and pain were there. They were simply reacting to that hurt. I don't blame them. So during a board meeting, it was decided that I and my family would have to leave, which we did, about eight months later. We left, and seven months later, after a horrendous car accident, we came back home. We could not get home off the brain. All we thought about was getting back home no matter what the cost. It didn't really make sense. Some wanted us gone and gone forever, but we wanted to be back there with them. I guess God was trying to prove what needed to happen. We returned, and then God began to restore things. Even with those who resented me the most,

God restored the friendship and relationship. In fact, they became some of my biggest supporters and biggest fans later down the road. I want to thank my church for allowing me and my family to continue to live and worship there during our process of restoration. First United Pentecostal Church of Augusta is one of the greatest churches I know and will be truly blessed for its participation in the ministry of restoration for years to come.

If you remember, the wicked witch could not get the shoes off of Dorothy. No matter what she tried, they stayed with Dorothy. I want to draw a parallel here. The shoes to Dorothy are the same as the anointing is to the failed leader. That's why the witch wanted the shoes and that's why the devil will always be after failed leaders. The anointing has the power to keep and take them back to the place they belong. They are anointed, and it cannot be removed from them, so no one witch or person can take that away. Another parallel is the dog. That's the ministry of the leader. Dorothy would not let go of the dog. There are going to be people throughout the leader's life that will try and take away the dog. It belongs to him, and it's up to him to keep it. Just a side note here, but if you spell *dog* backwards you get *God*. Don't you dare let go of him. He is all you need.

So, if you find yourself in the throes of a failed ministry and wondering if you should just run away and find a new home to hide in, or maybe you are a pastor looking for direction for what to do with the failed leader, I want you to remember one thing: There is just no place like home.

Chapter 12

House Arrest

In the last chapter, as you have read, I am completely in support of failed leaders not running from their homes and home church. I didn't, and it restored me even faster than expected. Mind you, I was the first of my kind at my home church, and so everything that was accomplished with me started as an experiment. Sure, we failed at times and had plenty of do-overs. But the fact remains, we did it right there under the scrutiny of those that wanted my head. And believe you me, they were watching, and if we stepped one way or the other outside the lines, they made us aware of our misstep rather quickly.

I want to tell you a story of a gentleman that lives in the western part of the United States. I will give you some of the details of his case; however, I will give a fictitious name to protect his now known innocence. Here is his story.

John was born in Detroit, Michigan, in 1980, to Gerald and Janice P. His father was a Finlander, a jack of all trades, but his main trade was carpentry. His mother is an African-American and was a Detroit police officer for twenty-five years. His parents divorced when he was five years old because of his father's heavy drinking, which he continued until his death in 2006. John came to the Lord through a high school friend of his brother's shortly before his sixteenth birthday. At the age of sixteen, he received the baptism of the Holy Spirit in a church in Rochester Hills, Michigan. Shortly after being born again, he realized a strong desire to witness to the lost and a love for the Word of God. During a church service, while musing in his heart whether he was called to preach, the Lord confirmed his thoughts by a "word of knowledge" given through an evangelist whom he had never seen prior to that service. The next two years were occupied with much prayer, fasting, and study. At times, his passion would be so stirred that he would leave home and walk the streets looking for someone to tell about Jesus. There was even a time he walked into a non-evangelical church and interrupted their board meeting to tell the pastor about Jesus and the cross.

After two years, things began to go wrong. With no support from home and the natural struggles of a young man, he began to backslide. Not too long afterward, he got involved in drugs and a completely sinful lifestyle. By the age of twenty-two, he had six juvenile arrests and four adult felony arrests. He had minor warrants in Arizona and Colorado, and a major warrant in Nevada. He went on the run and fled to Mexico for a year until the Lord brought him under strong conviction and began to deal with his heart. At this point, he told the Lord that he would serve him, and said the Lord spoke back to him and said he had to turn himself in to the authorities.

In November of 2001, he walked into a federal courthouse in Las Vegas, Nevada, and surrendered to the U.S. Marshals. After spending a few months in the city jail, the Lord assured him that he wasn't going to do the twelve years that his lawyer told him that he was facing. In July of 2002, he was sentenced to five years and eight months to a medium-high security prison in West Virginia. During his time in prison, he spent most of it seeking God, reading the Bible, and praying. He wrote to churches, soliciting study material which wasn't readily available in prison. He was able to get a Bible study with a teacher's manual and started teaching other inmates in the prison. After two years, he was transferred to a low security facility in Taft, California. In Taft, there was great liberty to pray and preach the Word. A great spirit of prayer developed there, and a revival began to take place throughout the prison. By the grace of God, a Spirit-filled chaplain was hired, which opened the door for more material and made it possible to baptize the inmates in Jesus' name. Before his release in 2007, he was privileged to see the prison go from no openly professing believers to a group of forty guys seeking salvation, and with the assistance of the chaplain, John was able to baptize twelve men.

Today, this man lives, breathes, and sleeps for the kingdom, but he is on house arrest. As a part of his probation, he has to report in and is being tracked by the authorities to be sure he stays within the lines. After being released, his current pastor, a man that believes in true restoration, recognized John's zeal and calling and asked him to join the ministerial staff there at the local church. John, however, not wanting to bring disgrace to the ministry, told his pastor that he did not want to do that while having to wear an ankle bracelet. His pastor responded with an amazing statement. He told him that the ankle bracelet only served the purpose of proving to others that there is such a thing as restoration to a fallen leader. He said it was a testimony that God can bring you back after you fall.

So today, John is basically on house arrest. His every move is being monitored. He prays, fasts, gives to God, and even preaches to the congregation all while wearing an ankle bracelet. He is on house arrest, and what better place to be arrested than in the house of God. All too often, when leaders fail, we ship them out, send them down the road, and basically tell them to hope for the best. It's time we start putting our failed leaders on house arrest. Keep them close to the place where people can watch and witness their restoration by the one who is in the business of restoring all things, Jesus Christ. The purpose of house arrest is to keep offending persons within a controlled environment so they will have the tools to become productive citizens again. Should we do any less with our failed leaders?

One of the biggest political questions of our day is what to do with the inmates being turned out into the general public after serving multiple years in prison. They face some of the hardest days ahead, becoming acclimated back into normal lives. They can hardly find jobs, and no one really wants to give them a chance. Today, there are countless ideals and programs underway, trying to figure out what to do and how to restore these people back into society. Many have failed and some are experiencing limited success. As the church, you will need to find some way, whether it be a mission statement, policy, or program to grab failed leaders and start the process of restoration. You can't just toss them out into the congregation. They will never last. They are so used to leading, guiding, and being the example that the crowd is a foreign place to them. Sure, they will need to sit down or step down from leading until they have fully given the situation over to God and allowed him to restore their hearts. Once this has taken place, fallen leaders will need to see that there is a plan, a process, and a place of hope that they will follow after until they have regained the trust and respect of people.

That is why I feel so adamant about keeping them at home. If the people never see them go through the process, they will have no idea what struggles and successes the failed leaders had to endure to get back to that place of honor. And unless people see it, they will never respect it. Never.

For this to work, I do understand that the church must be prepared and taught how to handle this type of thing. We will talk more about that later. But I do want to say this: there will be people in your church that will get upset. They will fuss and complain and take their spiritual potshots at you and the failed leader. You are going to have to accept in your mind that this is going to happen and whether or not it is worth it. These same people are the very ones who fuss over song books not being used or using too much technology in church services. All the while, they have the highest speed internet available in their homes so they can email the gossip about your attempt to restore a failed leader. They are already in great trouble and they simply do not understand the ministry that God has called us to. Therefore, they will never understand the purpose of restoration until they need restoring themselves. One day they will need it; then and only then will they get it. Just know in your mind that this thing is going to be hard. Just ask Jesus how hard it is to restore people back to relationship and purpose. If I have this correct, it took forty stripes, a crown of thorns, three nails, a spear, and a willingness to say, "Father forgive them for they know not what they do."

The fact remains that too many good leaders who made bad decisions and horrible mistakes are out there walking around in this world trying to fulfill their callings. They may find a temporary substitute, but always, at the end of the day, they will feel unfulfilled in their true purpose. We need to place them on house arrest.

Chapter 13

Wounds that Heal

Thus far, we have written about several cases of failed leadership and their subsequent return to full-time leadership. I have given you the case, both personal and Biblical, for restoration. I have a question that has been bouncing around inside my mind for several weeks. I wasn't sure how to eloquently bring it out on paper, so I will give you the rough version and you can deal with it from there.

When does restoration begin in the failed leader? Now, you are going to have to think about that a minute. The temptation is going to be to point to a visible event after they fall, or when they make their public declaration that they have not been whom they say they are. I ask you to stretch yourself a bit and really give this some thought before you cast your judgment or idea on when restoration actually starts.

I was reading a book a few years ago written by Mark Buchannan entitled, *Your God Is Too Safe*. I might add that it is one of the greatest books I have ever had the privilege to read. All of his books are amazing, for that matter, but this one just stuck with me. I think I ministered seven different sermons out of it and I am not finished yet. Kudos, Mr. Buchannan.

There is one particular chapter in his book that I would like to draw from in this section. Mark asked a question that just absolutely blew my mind; that kind of moment where when it all sank in I just sat in tears wondering what I was going to do with this new information. He asked the question, "Can these wounds heal?" He was speaking of the wounds that we give each other and the wounds that life tends to inflict upon us. He wasn't asking whether we can ever be healed of the wounds we receive or give. Rather, he was asking whether these wounds that we receive can heal us. That is a question that has turned my world upside down. Let's unpack this.

At conception, we are all given the temperaments that we will live with for the rest of our lives. God made us as he designed us to be. There is a theory out there that our temperaments have strengths and weaknesses. I do not believe that God does anything imperfectly. He makes us perfect, and because we are "shapen" in iniquity, our once perfect temperament becomes flawed by the environments we are exposed to. As this influence takes place, there are things that we pick up along the way that, combined with our temperament, creates these so-called weaknesses. This happens when our temperament needs are not being met. Even if you are raised in church all your life, there are going to be damaging influences planted within your heart. This deadly combination will ultimately lead us to wound others and also receive wounds.

But God has a plan. Have you ever noticed that for everything mankind goes through, God has always had a plan to deal with it? Great, isn't it? No matter what I am to become or have become, God has a plan that will ultimately lead me to perfection if I will let it. However, the process of our lives can really get ugly. Just to be honest, life can really suck at times and hurt badly. So, what do we do with these wounds? When will they heal or when will they heal us?

Several years ago, I was having a discussion with a friend of mine and as we discussed the paths that our lives had taken, the word *regrets* came into the conversation. As we contemplated this word,

I suddenly spoke without much thought and said, "I don't have any!" My friend just looked at me with this odd face, waiting for an explanation. As I searched for the words to explain, I said it again, "I don't have any regrets." He looked at me even more intensely than before. Then God began to speak to me and wrote it out for me in my mind. Before my failure, I was a mess. My friend nodded in confirmation. I thought, you jerk, you're not supposed to agree with that. No, just kidding. I continued. "Rodney, I was arrogant, egotistical, harsh, and sometimes unforgiving. I strived for excellence, not to be good at something, but so others could say I was good at it. My temperament, along with what environments I grew up in, created this need to be seen as better than the average. I had become a horrible person."

I was hard to be around, but because I had money, people would overlook the jerkish part of me and settle for what they could get. My family stayed around me because that is what families do. They stick together no matter what. However, there were times that they could have killed me, I know. But here is my revelation, thanks to Mark Buchannan. When I failed as a leader, people who once loved me kicked me out. They talked about me and ran me into the ground. They turned their backs on me and sought out rumors and lies. Each and every time that happened, I was cut and cut deeply. It created so many wounds that it literally changed who I was. Every wound moved me closer and closer to God in ways that I never knew existed.

What was happening to me? God was doing surgery on me and healing me every time I was cut by a friend or saint of God. How can that be, you say? Look at it this way. When a surgeon tells you that you have a bad heart and he needs to repair it, what comes next? Surgery, of course. Can they do heart surgery without cutting you? No, they can't. They literally cut you from your neck to just below your ribcage. They saw the sternum right down the middle and spread your chest apart. Anyone will tell you that the hardest part of open heart surgery is the recovery from the wound inflicted by the doctor when he cuts, saws, and spreads you open like a fish. I have never heard anyone tell anybody that their heart hurts after surgery. No, it's the wound created by the doctor to heal your busted heart that hurts so badly.

My failure and the subsequent wounds from people are what actually healed me and corrected my issues. Did it hurt? Of course, and I wish no one to go through what I did. But sometimes, the only way for God to heal someone is for them to fail, break down, and receive wounds that only the master can give or allow to be given. When the failure was all over, I was humble, loving, and caring of others like never before. Do I still struggle with issues? Yes, I do. But today, I deal with those issues behind the pain of wounds. Those wounds that I receive correct what is going on inside of me if I allow God to use them. *And we know that God causes everything to work together for the good of those who love God and are called according to his purpose for them* (Romans 8:28).

So I propose this thought to you. When a leader fails, is that not God doing surgery on them and trying to correct them? If so, and you throw them out on their ears because they failed, you are actually stepping into the process of God trying to fix them. You have walked into God's surgery room and shut down the power and taken away the tools he needs to complete the operation. Don't be responsible for shutting down God's OR.

God knows where every leader stands. He knows whether that leader is living up to the standards set by his word. He knows what it will take for that leader to become what he has designed for them to be. So the next time you see someone fall or you fall yourself, just remember, God may be in his OR. There is something that is on every OR door in every hospital in the country: a bright red stripe or sign that says, "Authorized Personnel Only." Why is that? I think the answer is simple enough, but we will state it anyway. The reason is because you do not have the qualifications to enter or the training and know-how to handle what happens in surgery. Stay out! You do not belong there.

So do you have wounds? I hope so. There is a really neat verse that I want to leave you with. *And one shall say unto him, What are these wounds in thine hands? Then he shall answer, Those with which I was wounded in the house of my friends* (Zechariah 13:6). Jesus received wounds from those he loved most. And it was because of these wounds that you and I today have healing and salvation. The wounds that he received made it possible for you and me to be here today. Wounds that heal, you better believe it.

For the Failed Leader

Chapter 14

First Things First—Character

One of the greatest deficiencies of leaders today is character. And the greatest question of all time is why. Character is that which you can rarely put your finger on in a person's life. It is the unseen guide in our lives. Let's face it. Has anyone congratulated you on your character lately? No one sees it, but they all experience it if they are around you for any period of time. John Maxwell, in his book, *Talent is Never Enough,* states that people are a lot like icebergs. Never have I heard a truer statement. What you see on the surface is just a small portion of what is most likely beneath. If the iceberg gets too large above the surface, it will not last and will topple over. A building can only be as tall as the foundation can handle. Build it too tall and it will not be stable, and the entire structure becomes a catastrophe waiting to happen.

Former President Bill Clinton made a statement once that his personal life should not be confused with his professional life. Never have I heard a more ridiculous and asinine statement. Your personal life will dictate how you conduct your professional life. Your personal life is what you are when no one is looking. Your professional life will only be guided by what you are on the inside.

I was listening to an interview of Dr. James C. Dobson with former Representative Newt Gingrich a few years ago. Dr. Dobson questioned him on this very subject. Apparently, Mr. Gingrich has had a few failed marriages and his faithfulness to his spouses had been in question. When asked about this, Mr. Gingrich gave the same reasoning as Bill Clinton. He felt that people should not judge him based on the mistakes he had made in his personal life while serving the American people. Both of these men feel that their personal lives have no relational consequence in their professional careers. I could not disagree more. What you are in your personal life will ultimately dictate and exemplify what you are or will become in your professional doings. There is no separation of the two.

Bill Clinton's legacy as a leader is forever tarnished because of his personal actions. Newt Gingrich lost a very powerful position in influencing American politics because of mistakes made in his personal life when they eventually unveiled themselves in his professional life. Both men paid hefty fines financially and morally. Today, neither have the same credibility as they did before their personal lack of character was exposed, and in large part, this is due to their commitment not to admit failure. Their stories, though they may be different in content, are no different than the thousands if not millions of leaders that failed before them and those that will fail after them. It all starts with believing that what we show people on the surface is all that matters. It has been said that you can fool some of the people some of the time, but you will never fool all of the people all of time. There is just no substitute for good character.

If a man is not faithful in his personal life, then how can he be expected to be faithful in his professional life? It is an absolute impossibility to do so. If you are a liar at home, you will be at liar at work. Proverbs 4:23 states, *Keep thy heart with all diligence; for out of it are the issues of life.* Our hearts contain the character of our lives. If the heart is corrupt, everything about us will become corrupt. The heart sends to the rest of the body life sustaining blood. If it is not functioning properly, then the entire body is subject to fail, organ by organ. Death is imminent. So it is with character.

If you are a leader who has failed, I am sure you can see what led to that failure. Simply put, it was a lack of character. Even if you have never failed in character matters before, if you fail, you fail in the arena of character. It may have taken years for it to be made known, but somewhere you lacked complete character. Now, everyone makes mistakes, but those mistakes are rooted in flawed character. Henry Parry Liddon said, "What we do on some great occasion will probably depend on what we already are; and what we are will be the result of previous years of self-discipline." Nothing you do today just happens by chance. It is the culmination of years of ingredients put into your life. Garbage in, garbage out. If you make self-discipline, values, and integrity your guide, you will refine and create in your person good character.

I have a question for you. Who are you? You are going to have to think about this for a while. Most of you right now are thinking, well, I am a professional. I am a lawyer, a preacher, a teacher, or a plumber. That's not what I asked you. I do not want to know what you do, but who you are. Maybe I should ask it this way: whose are you? It takes on a whole different feel when asked in that manner, doesn't it? When you wake up to the fact that you belong to God and you are his child, character means so much more. A person that believes that they do not belong to anyone becomes an island unto himself, and therefore is a law unto himself and cannot possess good character. Outside of God there is no moral compass (character). If I belong to him, then everything I do must represent whom I belong to. Most of us can handle making ourselves look bad, but it is a whole different thing altogether when we make someone else look bad. I think that is something that God just put into us, and it will grind away at our hearts if we sin like that.

When a leader fails, the first thing they should do is admit it. According to James 5, we should confess our faults one to another if we want to be healed. Now, you better be careful who you confess to, or you may find yourself in the middle of a horrible situation on top of the issues you have failed in. I believe a leader should always have someone (authority) they can confess their issues to. Accountability is the key. A leader should have an accountability partner that helps refine and complete good moral character in their lives. When I personally failed, I had no accountability partner. I was void of having someone keep me in line, even though I was an assistant to the pastor. My pastor was not good at holding people accountable, a major flaw in his leadership abilities, he admits today. But I became an island and therefore had no one to turn to. So, I did the only thing I could do; I confessed before the church. Oh yes, that was a major deal and they did not handle it well. It started a firestorm of rumors and caused great casualties among the people. In fact, today there is a man who still has not recovered from it. This is why it is so important to have an accountability partner who understands this verse in James 5. It never states to admit it before the church in whole, but it does direct us to find that person who understands and is able to restore you to healing. Galatians 6 tells us if we see someone fall that we should restore them in meekness, considering ourselves unless we, too, should fall in the same manner.

Character is so important. It takes character on both sides; both the sinner and the restorer must show good character for this to be successful. Failure in character in one matter does not allow us to fail in character in another.

If you have fallen as a leader, I beg of you to do the right thing. *Confess!* It will allow you to be restored to completeness. It will also allow your character to be repaired and made whole. Doing the right thing can be the hardest thing you will ever do, especially when you have already failed. George Washington said it best. "Few men have the virtue enough to withstand the highest bidder." If you confess and the person you confess to simply pats you on the back and says don't worry about it, something is very wrong. You need to find someone that will hold you accountable and work with you from that point forward to ensure that you are making proper steps toward rebuilding your character. As of this writing, I am working with a pastor that failed morally. Another pastor friend and I restored him and since have held him accountable. However, in the past few months, I have noticed that he has become very critical and judgmental of other leaders and organizations. What I noticed is that his criticism of others has been to cover up his own mistake for fear of exposure. He is trying to use his high standard and outspokenness to cover up the idea that he has fallen in any manner. His character is still flawed. So, I am working with him to show him that his character is the thing that is still not fixed. Any cover up of our own is not good character and is not godly. Only the blood of Christ can cover sin.

The Pharisees were professionals at covering their own sin. They simply created more laws and regulations to hide what they were doing. The more laws they created, the more spiritual they looked. Since creation, man has tried to create his own spiritual compass with immense failure. True character cannot be designed, created, or fashioned. Creation is over and has been since God rested on the seventh day. True character can only be built over time. Every issue, circumstance, and yes, failure can build character if you allow it. So, if you find yourself wondering what to do to become the leader you know God wants you to be, first things first, character.

Chapter 15

The Mark of a *Great* Man

The Bible is without doubt the most fascinating book ever written. Think about it. What book out there has ever stirred up so much controversy and yet has brought insurmountable peace to the masses at the same time? Today, books are written that either warm the heart or cause trepidation to the reader. But the Bible can do all of that in one brief recital of its holy writ. Never has a book been so scrutinized and yet stand so firmly the test of time. It transcends public opinion and the highest offices of law and was used as one of the foundational ingredients to form one of the greatest countries to ever exist. It has been on the bestseller list since they started tracking such a thing and has been regarded as an amazing phenomenon of all literature.

Inside its pages, it unveils the struggle of mankind with the law of God and the laws of nature that God created. Every story depicts the endless struggle of man to find out just who he really is. Many rise to greatness. Many fail. Some are just born and then die. We see however, that each left his/her fingerprint in this life so that those of us after them can take a peek and maybe learn something. In every single book of the Bible, you will see men and women doing their best to be the best that they can be. This was well before the U.S. Army came up with that slogan. And that is the greatest struggle unveiled in Scripture: men and women wanting, desiring, reaching, pulling, pushing, and fighting to be a success. It just seems to be a natural order of things for humans. Deep inside all of us resides the passion to be great. Color, creed, and nationality make no difference; we all want to be great and do great things.

Over time, the definition of greatness has changed considerably. Actually, it has changed throughout time, and I believe it fluctuates with society and culture. In ancient times, the leaders and architects of the Roman Empire were considered some of the greatest people to ever live. They formed a nation and culture out of nothing that is still present today. Today, though, greatness is nothing more than receiving a large contract to play sports professionally, or rising to the heights of corporate management with mega bonuses. It does not matter if you deal in drugs and endanger the lives of your fellow citizens; as long as you can throw the ball or create multi-million dollar mergers, you're considered great. And the strangest thing is that you can be paid millions regardless of your lack of morals. Think about it. Teachers in our school system are paid a pitiful wage for what they do. They are teaching and instructing our future leaders and they are hardly paid enough to survive. Police officers and military soldiers and others in public safety lay their lives on the line every day for our safety and they are not paid enough to live without having to obtain a second job. We call them heroes, but being a hero just does not pay the bills today. However, hit a golf ball over three hundred yards consistently and you can be a multi-millionaire. Throw a football downfield accurately and you will enter the hall of fame. Maintain a high batting average, with or without steroids, and you will be considered a person of greatness. Where did we go wrong?

In defining greatness, Webster's dictionary says this: "having or showing nobility of mind, purpose, etc." Take note: I used a collegiate edition dictionary printed in the 1950s. Now, with that defining statement, where is the nobility in our sports heroes? Where is the nobility in their purpose? However, I will be the first to tell you that hitting a golf ball over three hundred yards consistently in the fairway is quite a feat. It takes tremendous training and discipline. But does it really define greatness? I think Tiger Woods himself would tell you differently. I believe if you asked, he would tell you that what he does is not greatness, but is the result of hard work, training, and passion, and that mark in him was left by a man full of greatness, his father.

Update

Before I could get this book published, the airways and news bureaus were full of a story concerning Tiger Woods. Around the Thanksgiving holiday, a horrible and tragic story came out about one of golf's greatest players. The Tiger Woods we all loved and admired had a secret life and it was coming to the surface. According to all the buzz in the news, Tiger was leading quite the life contrary to what we thought or believed about a sports hero. It was brought to our attention that Tiger was just as much a human being as the rest of the people who lived around him. It is obvious that Tiger forgot the lessons taught him by his father. For nearly three months or so, Tiger disappeared from the public eye and then on February 19, 2010, he surfaced to make a public apology concerning his ordeal. In his apology to the world, he said some things that I felt were incredibly admirable, proving that he was a great man regardless of his failures. First of all, Tiger did not have to apologize to anyone but himself and his family. He owed no apology to the fans or the PGA. You may not agree with that, but really, he broke no rules of the organization, just the laws of morality and commitment to his God and family. Yet, he stood before countless millions apologizing for his behavior. He owned up to his mistakes. He took responsibility for them and he enrolled himself in counseling for the betterment of himself and his family. He stated that money and fame contributed to his failures as a man, a husband, and a father. (Matthew 16:26 [26] *And what do you benefit if you gain the whole world but lose your own soul? Is anything worth more than your* soul? NLT) *He went on to say that somehow he felt entitled to the things that eventually brought him down. That statement alone rocked my world! And there it is, the problem with our entire world. As we grow in fame and stature, we begin to feel entitled to what we call the good things of life. How many men or women have fallen walking down this same road? I think the numbers would pain us beyond our ability to comprehend. Once again, a great man in the eyes of the world falls, and yet when he stands before all and declares himself corrupt in repentance, the news hosts ridicule even his apology and question his return. Just more proof positive that we have it all wrong when it comes to greatness. Kudos, Tiger. I pray that not only do you return, but that you and your family will be stronger than ever.*

As we continue, I want to take you to the authority of greatness and find out what it says: The Bible. In 1 Kings 3, you will find the story of Solomon as he has just entered into kingship. It says that he has a dream that God asked him what he can give him. Solomon begins to thank the Lord for showing great kindness and mercy to his father, David, for allowing his son to inherit his throne. Solomon expresses his lack of confidence in the fact that he is but a child and does not know how to be kingly or act royally. In fact, he states that he does not even know how to walk in or out of a room as a king should. Let me say this right here. It is obvious that King David did very little to pass on to Solomon how he was to behave as a king. This is very sad, but applicable to us today. People all over this nation are upset with the behavior of our youth. We fuss and complain that youth know nothing of good character. However, what are *we* teaching our children? Are we teaching them how to act as royalty? The problem is not the youth. It is parents and leaders that are failing to teach our children how to walk in this life.

Solomon goes on to tell God how great the people are in number, and it becomes obvious Solomon is nervous in front of large crowds. Then he asks God for something unique. We have been taught all our lives that Solomon asks God for wisdom. I hate to break it to you, but that is incorrect. I am not telling you that your Sunday school teachers were wrong, but they did miss a most important clue. It is so easy to do, and I missed it for years until a pastor friend of mine made me aware of it. In verse 9, Solomon asks God for *an understanding heart*. Now, because we have recorded for us that Solomon used great wisdom in the tale of the two women with babies, we think that it was wisdom that he requested. Dig a little deeper with me for a moment. The Bible clearly states that he asks for an understanding heart. This understanding is defined in the Hebrew with the following:

OT:8085 shama` (shaw-mah'); a primitive root; to hear intelligently (often with implication of attention, obedience, etc.; causatively, to tell, etc.):

In today's language, it means to hear and obey. Solomon did not ask for wisdom to run the nation, he simply wanted a heart that could hear God's voice and obey what he says. That's why Solomon wrote in Proverbs 16:1, *The preparations of the heart in man, and the answer of the tongue, is from the Lord.*

So, what is the mark of a great man? We are taught from our births that we are to reach for the stars. Be the best you can be, we're told. Our military has given us the slogans of "Aim High," "Be All that You Can Be," and "We're Looking for a Few Good Men." We are told to get the best grades so we can attend the grandest institutions of higher learning available. Let no one hold you down. Shoot for the stars and reach the moon. We teach our kids that they can be anything they want to be. But inside of them there is a struggle with what we have instructed them to do. A dear friend of mine and I were talking one day about a young man from our city that had the ability to go to the University of Georgia and play football, but he chose to go to a lesser school and play. This confused me, and I made the statement, "How could he have made that kind of decision?" I, too, realize now that even my way of thinking is after this pattern. Go for the best. Why would you not?

I suppose that all the above slogans and quotes are in order. I want my kids to be successful. I want them to achieve the finest that life can offer. I want them to be as successful as one can be without trading in the values given us in the Word of God. So we do our best to point them in the right direction. We use men of the Bible that were truly great men of God. King Saul was one of those great men. The Bible declares him as such. *And he had a son, whose name was Saul, a choice young man, and a goodly: and there was not among the children of Israel a goodlier person than he: from his shoulders and upward he was higher than any of the people* (1 Samuel 9:2). Saul was a man that stood head and shoulders over them all. He was the best he could be. It appeared that Saul had the "mark of a great man." He was a great warrior and led Israel to many successful missions in keeping their land and nation together. We all know the story of how Saul messed up later and God rejected him as king over Israel. God made him a *great man* in the eyes of many and he did many *great things,* yet he still lacked something.

God, through the prophet Samuel, gave King Saul instruction for King Amalek and his stuff. He was supposed to kill him and all the people with him. However, he thought it better to come back with the spoils. When Samuel arrives to meet King Saul, he hears the bleating of animals and notices a strange king. He says this to King Saul: *And Samuel said, Hath the Lord as great delight in burnt offerings and sacrifices, as in obeying the voice of the Lord? Behold, to obey is better than sacrifice, and to hearken than the fat of rams* (1 Sam 15:22). If God takes *a greater* delight in *obedience* than he does in how much one sacrifices, then the "mark of a great man" is not how much he sacrifices or how much he does or even what he does, but only rests within his obedience to God and his laws.

This is where many leaders run into trouble. We strive so hard for greatness in what we do that we forget the most valuable part of leadership: obedience to the one who put us in leadership. Please understand me here. I believe you should be the best you can be and train well and train hard. But there is no substitute for obedience to the Word of God. Why do we try so hard to be successful? I believe part of it is that we are too preoccupied with pleasing people. Another reason is that as leaders, it is part of our makeup. We seem to have a natural drive that, left unchecked, can lead us down roads of compromise. Early in my life, I left a family business because I felt I was treated unfairly with the wage they paid me. So, I went out on my own to prove that I could be a success without them. Later, I did become that success. I was very successful by most standards. I lived the dream life. However, I disobeyed a valuable law in the Word of God. Romans 12:3 tells a man *not to think of himself more highly that he ought to think, but think soberly.* That was my sin first. I began to think about myself in ways that broke this principal. The result was compromise. As leaders, we must die to ourselves. This is a concept not accepted in our culture. We are told to let no one rule us and we are the gods of our own worlds. I guess that is true with most. If we are gods of our own world and we think that we are that good, then why is our world such a mess? The answer is painfully obvious. We just think we are gods and that good. Again, Scripture beautifully applies. *Only the Lord give thee wisdom and understanding, and give thee charge concerning Israel, that thou mayest keep the law of the Lord thy God* (1 Chronicles 22:12).

There is a powerful story in Scripture that speaks of obedience. Matthew chapter 8 unveils the story. A centurion's servant is sick and is in great torment due to his disease. Jesus quickly responds that he will come and heal him. However, the centurion says something that most likely shocked everyone standing within earshot. He states that he is not worthy for Jesus to come to his house, but that he only need speak the word and that will be good enough. He then gives reason to his madness. In verse 9 his says, "For I am a man under authority." He then tells Jesus that he has soldiers under him and whatever he tells them to do, their obedience to his word gets the job done. In other words, I know the power of obedience because I've seen it work. Where there is no obedience there is no authority. God cannot lead you if you cannot obey. In fact, I will go as far as to say that God and his Word are powerless unless you obey.

Here is the best part. When Jesus heard what the centurion said, he marveled. Jesus then says the he has not heard "so great a faith in all of Israel." Now, was the faith that Jesus marveled at the faith that the centurion believed that Jesus could heal the servant without even going to see him? Look closer. The faith that Jesus marveled at was the faith that was directly tied to this man's understanding of the power of obedience. Let me say it this way. You cannot have true faith without true obedience. One cannot exist without the other. Show me a person that lacks faith, whether momentarily or consistently, and I will show you a person that is not obedient in some form or fashion. It is a universal law. I feel I need to explain this a bit further. Why do we break the speed limits established in our country on the highways we travel? Could it be that we do not believe (faith) the speeds that the authorities have set for us are fast enough? That is exactly the issue. We lack faith in our government. Why did we break the rules that our parents set for us as children? Because we did not believe (faith) that they were correct in doing so. No wonder our generation is considered such a faithless (disobedient) generation. We break all the rules and cross all the boundaries and believe only in ourselves. Yet never before have we made a more devastating pursuit.

We have heard it for most of our lives. Absolute power corrupts absolutely. Somewhere we must come back to the understanding that we need God in our lives. Not just in our lives, but total surrender to his Word. I desperately want to do great things. I don't think that I will ever not desire that. But today, after blowing it badly, so many times, greatness, I now know, is not found in what we call greatness today, but is only found in an obedient heart. Have you ever wondered why King David was chosen by God, even after he blew it so horribly? In Acts 13:22 we find: *I have found David the son of Jesse, a man after mine own heart, which shall fulfill all my will.* Paul was speaking to the men of Antioch. He said that God had found a man after his own heart. Do you know what the heart of God is? Have you ever experienced his true heartbeat? In the case you are finding yourself in the same place that I did, I found a one more verse for you. *And being found in fashion as a man, he humbled himself, and became obedient unto death, even the death of the cross* (Philippians 2:8).

Now I think you know why he chose David. It was the ability to die unto one's own self. So then, the "mark of a great man" has three nail prints and a pierced side. By the way, where is your mark (cross)?

Chapter 16

I Am a Leader

I am a leader. I am strong. I am a visionary and I am a thinker. I was called for this and I can take it. I have in me the things that belong to a leader. I was told from a young age that in me were the qualities of a leader. People need me. People like being around me. Leadership comes easily to me. I enjoy it and I live for it. When I am not leading, I feel like I am not living. Leading is my passion, my desire, my ambition, my confirmation, and my love. I want to be a strong leader, a confident leader, a passionate leader, and an effective leader. I live for leadership.

But,

I am hurting, I am broken, and I am desperate. I sit in a church service looking, longing, and seeking the answers to the questions that no one knows are there in my heart. I hurt; I ache to be more than I currently am. I change seats; it doesn't work. I take on new projects; it doesn't work. I volunteer for more tasks; it doesn't work. I hurt. I am lost, confused, and delirious. I feel after God in the dark, unable to touch him. I pray the same words over and over, not knowing what to say next. I hurt and I don't know why. I just feel bad and I don't know why. I wake each morning just knowing that the days that were before are now over and I will be back; it doesn't work. I look in the mirror each day knowing that the man I see is not the man trapped inside. I want out, but I can't get out.

But,

I am a leader and I can take it. This is why I am a leader, because I am chosen to suffer and stand tall without wavering. So for now, I will take it. I will stand and I will not waver. I hurt, but you will not know it. I am in pain, but I will not show it. If you ask, I will just tell you that I am tired. Rough week, long week, but God is good is what I will say.

But,

I sit in a prayer meeting with other leaders. Sounds of blessing and walking with God are all around, yet I see nothing, I feel nothing. My soul screams for relief, but no rescue for me. I am surrounded by leaders, not one of whom hears my cry or feels my pain. Is it that God has put me here on my own, or can they not hear from him either, to know my hurt?

But,

Is that not what leaders do? We hurt alone, we walk alone, and we cry alone. If I must, I will do so alone.

But,

I am a leader, I am strong, and I am ... *not.*

Chapter 17

I Am but a Child (leader)

I wrote the "I am a Leader" chapter in the middle of a prayer revival at our church in Augusta, Georgia. Our church had never participated in anything like that before, but it was unique and interesting. Let me give you a little background into my life at that time. Earlier in the year of 2008, I felt that there was a tremendous economic downturn coming that would affect my business, so I started trying to make plans to secure its future. Although, I did so without a lot of input from God, mainly because I really did not ask him, come to think of it.

One of my clients made a suggestion of partnering or merging the companies together to help in sustaining both firms and giving us a competitive edge in our market. Things began to move quite quickly and everything seemed to just fall in place. I even remember making the statement that it sure felt like a God thing, regardless of the fact that I knew I had not really asked God much about the situation. As we sat down at the table, it went even faster. All the while, my stomach had that funny feeling, screaming, "Don't do this!" and "This is a very bad idea!" But hey, I am a leader and I know how to plan and I know how to lead into the future. We signed the deal.

From the first month, things started to go wrong. Every month was met with new unexpected challenges and not the good kind of challenges, either. The rules contained within the contract began to change, and they did so all the way up until things just exploded into turmoil. The people I partnered with were not willing to pay us the money they said they would and began to make unreasonable and undoable requests. Now I understand that they were just trying to push me out. But the more important thing was that these two women who I partnered my company with were living alternative lifestyles completely contrary to my beliefs and relationship with God. Talk about being "unequally yoked."

Up until the day of signing the deal, I had only met the principals once and thought then that something was different, but I just did not want to be judgmental. The fact was that I had no business being partners with them, but I ignored that small, still voice in my heart. Oh, did I mention that the Bible does have a lot to say about being unequally yoked? Well it does, but I chose to ignore that also.

So here I am in a mess with no way to get out, it seems. Then the door opens. It was not the kind of door that I would have liked to open, but I can't say that I have had a great track record of walking through the right doors anyway. There is a truth that I heard Andy Stanley address in one of his talks at Catalyst. He said just because the door opens does not mean it is the right door for you to walk through. Sometimes it will look, smell, and even feel like the will of God, but has absolutely nothing to do with God. That door that I chose to walk through was a really bad choice.

After refusing to comply with a request of these two women, they locked me out of my email, called the contract void, and tried to enforce a non-compete agreement to keep me out of the business. They contacted all my clients and told each of them that I was no longer with the company and they were now in control. Right then and there I lost 50 percent of my income. I was also contracted through them with a utilities company for a completely different type of business, and out of retaliation, they fired me from that contract as well. There goes the other 50 percent of my income.

Now let me break it down for you. I lost my company and job, all of my income with two cars, a house, two kids, and a wife to care for. Oh no, I was not feeling much like a leader. The quote kept coming to my mind that leaders don't lead when things are good, but when things get bad, the real leaders step forth. I wish I could align myself with that, but it just escapes me. I will explain later, but before I do, it gets better. Not only has all this stuff hit my home, but our church is also in a major transition and I have just been elected to the church board as administrator/treasurer of our church. Oh yeah, the leader who cannot listen to God about business issues is getting ready to take over the business issues of his house. Is that not great comedy or what?

Now back to the prayer revival. Here I am, sitting in this revival with all this mess going on in my life, and I can feel nothing. I am begging God to help me and I want to pray and I want to talk to God, but I keep uttering the same five words over and over again. Nothing I try to say makes sense. I can't articulate anything I am thinking into words to him. My mind is screaming, you can do this, you are a leader! I mean, out of fifteen leaders in the church, I was one of seven that showed up. Does that not count for something? As I sat there in spiritual pain, my body began to ache all over to the point that I developed one of the biggest migraines ever. I was hurting.

So it was there that I began to write the "I am a Leader" piece. I could not vocally say those things, so I thought I would write them. As I reached the end of that rant, it suddenly occurred to me that the whole issue was that I was trying too hard to be a leader and not trying at all to be just one of God's kids. That is why I ended it with "I am a leader ... *not.*"

I would dare say that this is a major problem with most leaders, but since that would be casting a large net, I will digress and just say that this is my problem. God has called me to be a leader, but when it comes to my relationship with him, I am only called to be one of his kids. When I am leading a group of people, teaching a class, running the multimedia, or preaching a sermon, I am a leader. But when I pray, fast, and read God's Word, I am just one of his. I must check my leadership at the door because now I am in his presence and no other leader is needed. If you could look back over your life and notice that when you would go to church, pray in that service, and worship, you were doing so from a leadership perspective and not as a child. I guess that is why he said to "suffer the little children to come unto me." And then he went on to say that "such was the kingdom of God." Even though we are leaders and called to be so, he wants us as children, because then and only then can he be our Father and do the things for us and with us he desires to do.

I have to ask you this question. Is this not where you go wrong? Being a leader, if you are a true leader, will take you here every time if you are not careful. As leaders we just set the course and go. We feel the direction and purpose in what we do, so why would we stop to be anything less? There is the mistake. Our first calling is just being one of his kids. Our second calling is being the leader that he has designed for us to be. As children, we trust everything our parents tell us. Then we grow up. In the beginnings of our leadership path, we trust everything our mentors and pastors tell us, and then we grow up. We lose touch with what got us where we are and start trusting our own knowledge and intellect. We can possess all the knowledge of leadership that there is, but if we fail to check with one who created that knowledge, we will ultimately misinterpret that knowledge.

When you look at leaders who fail, what is the one thing that you say? "How could they have been so stupid?" You do, don't you? Why? Because from the outside, we can see the issues without the cloudiness of the situation. We say things like if I ever reach a position like that, then I will be so careful and I … Do you get it? You already committed the sin and you are not even there yet. It all becomes about *me*. If I had that job, if I had the position, if I had that money, I would do … As leaders, we are prone to act and think like we have the answers. But as kids, we know we don't and we are not afraid to ask questions. Real leadership is not having all the answers, but knowing where to find them.

Earlier, I brought to the discussion the quote that true leaders show up not in good times but show themselves strong in the rough times. Again, I just can't seem to reconcile that in my mind. When we think of this quote, we imagine a stoic-looking character marching to the top of the hill to view a bad situation. He looks like G. I. Joe. Well, maybe not, but you get the picture. We see him making command decisions and putting the proper people and resources in play, and then the problem is solved. Maybe that happens in Hollywood or in fictional books, but not in real life. Sure, there are talented leaders who have accomplished impressive things with limited resources, but most of the time, the truth is that we all have faced issues we just could not get a grip on. We failed, we missed the mark, and it just blows our minds how we could have been so wrong. The point is that I believe the true leader, when things get rough, doesn't just show up, but they fall before God like a child and ask him for the answers. And when he speaks, they act. That is the essence of true leadership. The fact of the matter is that on our best day we are undone before God, and all the leadership skills we may hold pale in comparison to his wisdom.

Every leader will be faced with what looks like insurmountable odds at some point in his/her life. Sometimes it is of our own doing and sometimes it is just what life throws at us. However, if we can understand that our leadership had its beginnings in God and will only prosper if it stays with God, then and only then will we ultimately see success. If you are a leader, you will struggle with believing more in your own abilities than in God's. It really is a natural progression. Most of us don't mean for it to happen, but it does.

A true negative result of the litmus test for this is to have something come against you that you can do absolutely nothing about and your response is to start freaking out and trying your best to work out of it. I will use myself as an example, because in this area I have failed miserably, and it took my daughter of eleven years of age at the time to reveal it to me. When the business deal I entered into went bad and my ex-partners started calling my clients, it shook me to the core. There was not one thing I could do to stop them from doing what they were doing and it drove me absolutely bonkers. As I drove down the highway in my newly purchased Mercedes-Benz (that now I could not pay for), I would scream into the air about what they were doing to me. I would call my wife looking for support in my desires to take them out. I wanted them dead! That's just how hard this thing hit me. The more I tried to calm my clients, the more phone calls, faxes, and certified letters they would send out trying to steal my clients from me. As a leader, I did everything I could and failed. So, I tried to do even more. The more I tried to combat and fix things, the more I had to fight spiritually. What was happening? It was God trying to show me that my leadership skills were not enough. I still needed him! Why is it with leaders that we must make God take us there? Why can't we get it from the start as young leaders and stay with the mindset that we will never outgrow God in our need for him? Maybe you have, but for me and most leaders I know it takes years of wrestling with God before we succumb to his touch. Story sound familiar? It should. Jacob, our spiritual bloodline of leadership, did the very same thing. He learned, led, and connived his way to the top until God arrested his leadership to receive his blessing.

I want to submit to you a letter from my daughter that she gave to me during the time I was fighting the bad business practices of two very nasty people. When I read it, I cried. I read it again and I cried more. I read it again and felt so small. If this does not get to you, nothing will. I have inserted this letter into the book in her original handwriting so as to set the stage of just how heartfelt this little girl's message was to her daddy.

I love you so much Daddy your my everything
you have such a impact on my life.
When i get older i want to be just like you,
you never need 2 worry bout money or
losing the house or car cause as long as i
live you will never lose me. I will always
Be your little Girl♥ But i want my
old daddy Back the one who always trusted in
God for everything and never stressed
Because you knew that God had it onder
control. It's time for you to get in
the passengers seat and let God stere the
car, I love you♥ never forget that
               Love,
               Daddy's little Girl.

It is okay if you have stained these pages with tears at this point. I honestly hope you do. This letter has been with me ever since. I carry it with me every day and wherever my travels with my company take me. I often read this for devotions before the day starts. As of writing this book, I am planning to frame a copy to put on my office wall for a reminder of just whose leader I am and what I am not. I don't know if you noticed it or not, but she makes a comment that I thought was pretty sneaky. She said I did not have to worry about losing her as long as she lived. I know it is not true, because the fact is that she will marry some man-child jerk because she will be confident in knowing what a true leader is by remembering that Daddy took his hands off the steering wheel of leadership and let God do the driving. She will know what true leadership looks like, feels like, and lives like because of what I do with my leadership before her now.

As leaders, it is so easy to forget who should actually be driving the car. It is so easy to forget just who gave us the talent to lead and who the people we are leading belong to. For me it, took a little girl to bring her all grown up daddy (leader) to remembrance of what he is *not*.

Chapter 18

The Secret Place

As I began to write this chapter, something unique happened. I started typing the title and my Word program underscored the words *Secret Place* with a smart tag. This may not seem unusual to you, but I was intrigued with the fact that even Microsoft indentified the title of this chapter as a real place that very well may have an address. I guess I am amused by the smallest of things. However, interestingly enough, it was a small confirmation that this place really does exist, at least with Microsoft and myself.

I have a secret to tell, and if you have never heard this before, it is going to come as a big shock to you. Everyone has secrets. Yep, we all do. I would also say that everyone is hiding something from someone else. Now, I don't want you to feel bad about it, because secrets seem to be a part of life. If you have lived for any amount time, you have secrets or you are well on your way in developing them. There are secrets about ourselves, our parents, our friends, our jobs, our relationships, our actions, our thoughts … I think you get the point. Secrets are a great part of our lives.

The only problem I have with secrets is that they are very negative. Can you think of one good (positive) secret (about yourself) that you are holding on to? Of course you can't, because if we are being honest, we admit that we won't let one good thing go unspoken about ourselves. Again, secrets by nature are a very negative thing, generally speaking. *Dictionary.com* describes *secret* as something that is or is kept secret, hidden, or concealed. We would be embarrassed and ashamed to know if anyone were to find out the secret things of our lives. Now, obviously there are things that we keep private due to the nature of them, but that is different from secrets we hold close to the vest.

What is the big deal about secrets? If you have been to the grocery store lately you will see a host of news articles revealing what so many believe to be secrets and making big money on them. Why? Because we all love a good secret that has been exposed. We love the shock and awe of them. We really get into the juiciness of the tale. In fact, the meatier the story (secret) the better it will sell. Our nations spy on each other because we just have to know what the other is doing and we hate not knowing what is going on behind closed doors. Many people have been able to sell out their country for big bucks because people love secrets.

As I already mentioned, we are enamored with hearing a big secret, and the church world is no different. I think it actually may be a bit more intense when you think about it. Nothing stirs more passion in a local church than for congregates to find out that one of theirs is hiding a big secret. If they happen to be in leadership, you better look out. That secret is going to spread faster than a California wildfire. It will swoop down on every level of that church and render it paralyzed for weeks to months before it recovers. However, I just don't get it. If I recall, Romans 3:23 says that all have sinned and made a royal mess of it. With that being said, what is the big deal about finding out that your brother or sister has some pretty big secrets bouncing around in their heads? If the Scriptures are true, and no one has uncovered that they are not, and with this Scripture giving us this warning, why then does it take us by surprise? I want you to really think about it. Your music director, youth pastor, Sunday school teacher, and oh yes, the deacon board and your senior pastor, they all have some really big secrets.

If we have anything in common, this is it. We sin and we have secrets. But there is one more thing that we all have in common. We all hate having secrets. Not one of us like moving about our lives carrying these secret issues. It drives us crazy, and for some it makes this life a living hell. There is no depth to which our secrets stop. We hide secrets from our friends, our co-workers, our kids, and our spouses. We sometimes think we even hide them from God. We sit in our churches, wishing for a way to release these things and let them float away with the sounds of the next chorus. We hang on every word from the minister, hoping that there is some nugget of truth that will attach itself to our secrets and drop them into the sea of forgetfulness.

Can you imagine waking up one morning and coming to the realization that all your secrets were gone? Can you imagine waking up and there was nothing about yourself to hide? There is such a place. But before I take you there, I want to share something that I got from a Christmas movie I was watching the other day.

In the hit movie, *The Santa Clause 3: The Escape Clause*, starring Tim Allen as Claus, there has developed a major problem. Mrs. Claus is pregnant. No, that is not the problem. However, the real problem is that Mrs. Claus really wants to see her parents, who, by the way, are very bitter with her husband for taking her away. But she is stuck at the North Pole. She is in no shape to travel and there are no phones connected to the outside world, so she can't call and is stuck there without any hope of things changing, at least in the immediate future. Santa comes up with a great solution: "We will bring them here." But that can't happen because there is a secret that they are all trying to keep. Tim Allen's character is Santa, and her parents, along with the rest of the world, can't know this.

So, the grand scheme is created to change the entire look of the North Pole and turn it into Canada. They change buildings, signs, and anything that would give the slightest hint that the North Pole does exist. All of the elves change clothes and wear toboggans to hide their pointy ears. It truly is a major thing hiding this secret. Santa travels to the States with Mr. Sandman and they put the unknowing in-laws to sleep. Not a bad idea, I must admit. Just kidding. I love my in-laws, really I do. So off to the North Pole—I mean Canada—they go.

They get there and all things seem to be working out, but as in every case, there is someone there who is intent on exposing this little secret. It appears Jack Frost is really upset with Santa and desires nothing more than to expose him for the liar he has been. As Jack Frost sabotages the process of keeping this secret, things began to go very wrong. Equipment is failing, Santa is becoming a jerk, and Mrs. Claus is reconsidering her commitment to the North Pole. All the while, the in-laws are becoming more aware that things are not as they seem. Then it happens. Santa is tricked into speaking the words that should never be spoken: "I wish I had never been chosen to be Santa."

In an instant, Santa is removed as Santa and he is transported back into his old life where things are horribly wrong. He is divorced. His only child hates him and he somehow managed to break up his ex-wife's current marriage, and she really hates him now if it was not enough before. And to boot, the North Pole is turned into an amusement park, corrupted by the commercialization of Christmas rather than being the place of those wonderful dreams of hope and trust. And why? All to protect a secret.

As Tim Allen's character, Santa, walks around, he sees what he has done. He forfeited his rightful place of his calling to protect a secret that should have never been a secret. So as all movies do, he sets out to create a happy ending. He manages to get back into the Santa suit and reconnect with his calling. However, this time he exposes the little secret he tried so hard to protect. He shows the family that he and his wife are, in fact, the Clauses and they are really located at the North Pole. Then little elves reveal themselves for who they really are, and the North Pole becomes alive again, creating those hopes and dreams for all the children of the world. The relationship between Santa and his in-laws is restored, and all things are made perfect again at the North Pole. The exposing of a secret leveled the playing field for all there.

You may ask yourself if this story is relevant to us in the ministry. Only you who hold the secret of your life can answer that. I can tell you it has been relevant for me. I don't go around trying to be something that I am not anymore. Yes, I failed, and failed miserably, as I have shared with you. But today, I use my failure to help others. I count on Romans 8:28 to hold true for me. I know all things will work together for my good. I have no reason to hide any secrets. Exposing secrets can be a very scary thing, but it can also be liberating. Now, before you get too dramatic and messed up with this thought, I want to clarify some things.

I am in no way suggesting that you stand up before a congregation and expose all the dirty little secrets you have been holding on to. Your church will not likely be able to handle that correctly. Few churches today have reached that level of maturity. I have had the distinct pleasure of attending a church that was and they are awesome. It is a calling that is very unique, but costly. However, I would never suggest that you give details about your failure. Just suffice it to say that we need not act like we have never fallen. That is where we get into trouble. We should allow people to know that we have fallen and that they, too, can be restored. Our testimony is the only thing that can help sometimes. If they understand that someone else has made mistakes and they, too, can recover, it will give them hope in a time when all hope appears to be lost.

I was attending a church service where there was a man that had a bad ordeal happen in his home. He and his wife were pastoring a great church in North America. However, things went horribly wrong with their relationship. Soon, they were separated and resigned the church. However, he quickly met another woman and was married. Well, as you can guess, this started a firestorm of rumors. He was accused of having an affair with this woman before his divorce. That may or may not have been true, but nonetheless, he married her. His ministerial organization branded him, and he resigned his credentials with them. For the next few years, he faithfully attended a church with his new family, but sat there with bitterness. He was cantankerous and moody. Every other word from him was laced in bitterness and anger.

Then it happened. He was overshadowed by God concerning his issue. He realized he was trying his best to cover up a secret. He was blaming everyone else for this issue when all along, it was the secret that kept him bound. He went to his pastor and confessed his issue. Did he give details? No. He simply confessed he was wrong and had been wrong. Then about a week later, he was given an opportunity to speak in a midweek service. He was not preaching, but just sharing some thoughts with the church as requested by the pastor. I was so proud of him. Instead of acting like he had it all together, he stood up and confessed. He did not give the details of his failure. He simply stood up and confessed that he had failed, he had been a jerk, and that his spirit had been wrong. Case closed. The church stood up on their feet and clapped their hands with such emotion I thought the building was going to lift off the ground. What happened? A secret was exposed inside the presence of a forgiving God.

Psalm 91:1 says, *He that dwells in the secret place of the Most High shall abide in the shadow of the Almighty.* As I said before, this secret place does exist and it is very real. The very idea of this verse is abiding with God and being in the same place as God keeps his home. If you have sinned, and if you are breathing you *have* sinned, then there is no better place to be than in his house. But, our normal response is that when we blow it and blow it majorly, we usually run the other direction. The church has, in the past, put such shame to those that fall that they feel they can't go to the one place we should be running to. The word *abide* here literally means to sit or sitting in the secret place. This gives me a visual of literally stopping my running, sitting down, shutting up, and listening to him. I am now resting in his house so he can heal me. It says when I stop running, then I will abide "under the shadow of the Almighty." I will abide under his watchful eye and his unfailing protection.

Psalm 27:5 says, *For in a time of trouble he shall hide me in his pavilion; in the secret of His tabernacle he shall hide me; he shall set me upon a rock.* Regardless of what the self-righteous folk think, I know no better place than the house of God to run when I fall and make mistakes. However, the biggest issue is that we are too concerned with the reputation of the church, and that is why our people who fall so easily walk away. It is almost as if they inherently understand and know that's what will be required of them. However, I have great news. That is not required, and God does not want that to happen to you. *In the covert of thy presence wilt thou hide them from the plottings of man: Thou wilt keep them secretly in a pavilion from the strife of tongues* (Psalm 31:20). If we as leaders and the people of the church would work toward restoring those that fall as hard as we work on telling the tale, we would have less backsliding in our congregations.

Now, I know some of the thoughts that are going through your mind. "Is that not the consequence of sin?" "Is that not what happens when you mess up?" and "Is that not the punishment?" Sure it is, if you do not run to the secret place. All of that will apply and more. But from the Scripture point of view, when I am in the secret place, God protects me from those things. Not convinced? Let's look at one of my favorite verses. *Thou art my hiding-place; thou wilt preserve me from trouble; Thou wilt compass me about with songs of deliverance* (Psalm 32:7). Again, the idea is that we are safe under his protection. The initial understanding is that we are concealed from the enemy. However, the reference, as made in verse 1 of this chapter, is that of sin. David is saying that God is the hiding place when I sin and he will protect me from the consequences of sin. By running to God, he will keep back all the evils caused by my sin.

As in the story of *The Santa Clause 3,* there will always be someone that desires to expose whatever dark secret you are hiding. Satan will always attempt to expose you for who you are and embarrass you, because he knows that is the church's biggest weakness. The best way to stop that is to confess. Again, I am in no way saying that public confession is the thing to do here. But you should confess to your pastor or someone that is accountable for you. This normally puts the squash on the ability of the enemy to create the rumors.

I have a question for you about the whole secret place thing. What makes the secret place the secret place? What makes it so safe? What makes this place a place of protection and security? It is the revealing of secrets. That's right; the revealing of secrets is what makes the secret place the secret place. When I go to God and tell him everything that is hidden in my heart, it releases God to cover me and protect me. Salvation is not a requirement for you. You can be saved if you want to or you can be lost. It's really your choice. God will never force this thing upon you. I know there are arguments out there that say, "Well, God died for everyone." That is true, but he never makes you accept it. If you are truly convinced to jump off a bridge, there is nothing I can do to make you come down. I can show you how to come down and show you the need to reconsider your options, but I can't make you. It is a personal decision that you must be willing to consider for it to have an effect. And the hiding of your sin is no different. God will not do anything until you are willing to confess it. *If we confess our sin, he is faithful and able to forgive us (hide us),* emphasis mine.

Choosing to tell God all that is in my heart does in fact allow God to cover and protect me from my failures. When you confess, it stops that merry-go-round of hiding the sin you committed. The more you try to hide, the more schemes you have to come up with to keep it concealed. Every day of your life, you will be confronted with your failures in some form or fashion. The only way to cover and hide sin is to allow the blood of Christ to cover it completely.

So, if you find yourself in the middle of the storms of your failure and needing protection, go to God and confess it, then go to your pastor and confess it again. When you do, you will find yourself in the greatest place a person can be, the Secret Place.

Chapter 19

You Have to Want It

I am going assume that you read chapter eight. If not, stop right here and go back and read it. If you can't remember it, read it again. I will see you when you get back.

Oh good! You're back! Let's proceed.

The success of both the lady caught in the act of adultery and Peter has, in large part, to do with their willingness to accept what Jesus did for them. Jesus dealt with the forgiveness and covering of their sins. It was now up to both of them what they would do with such a pardon as they were given. I realize that most of the religious world is not in favor of restoring failed leaders. It is, however, a growing movement that the church can no longer ignore. But regardless of whether the church wants to restore its failed leaders, it is not the church's choice to forgive them. It is the church's duty!

As a failed leader, sometimes you are harder on yourself than the church can be. Sometimes. I know there are leaders that act like because they have the belief that Jesus forgives and forgets that this gives them license to sin. They could not be more wrong. But, there are those leaders that feel they are no longer worthy to serve God as a leader. We have already discussed these issues, and I hope it opens a great deal of dialogue, but we will not go back over it. The fact is that as a failed leader, you have got to want the restoration. A false sense of punishment and/or penalty is not going to pay for the mistake you made. Nothing you do and no amount of time of absence from leadership is going to make up for the wrongs. That is not your job. Jesus did all of that at the cross. So go ahead and make up in your mind that there is nothing *you* can do, but Jesus has already completed that task. Just allow this understanding of what Christ has done for you to keep you from this point forward and never forget it.

In 1829, George Wilson of Pennsylvania was sentenced to be hanged by a United States court for robbing and murdering postal workers. However, for whatever reason, President Andrew Jackson pardoned him. But the pardon was refused by George Wilson. Wilson insisted that it was not a pardon unless he accepted it. That was a point that had never been addressed. So the President called on the Supreme Court to decide. Chief Justice John Marshall gave the following opinion of the Court:

"A pardon is a piece of paper, the value of which depends upon its acceptance by the person implicated. It is hardly supposed that one under sentence of death would refuse to accept a pardon, but if refused, it is no pardon. George Wilson must be hanged."

And he was.

Chapter 20

Just One More Time

It was the summer of 1999, and we were having the time of our lives on Clarks Hill Lake near Augusta, Georgia. Earlier that year, my wife and I purchased our first boat, which soon became our second home. Every chance we got, we were on the lake. As I stated in the first chapter, we named our boat *Visitation*. Just in case people wanted to know where we spent most of our time, we were able to tell them we were on *Visitation*.

Wesley McClain, affectionately called Uncle Wesley, wanted to introduce us to the world of water sports. We started out with tubing, then we went to the kneeboard, and then he decided that it was time to graduate to the wakeboard. Of course we were game, and after some rather expensive purchases, we were off to the lake.

We started midmorning that June, with just a slight ripple in the water, perfect water for this type of sport. Since Uncle Wes was the teacher, he would be first. After some struggle to get the boots on and locked into the correct position, he was thrown overboard. The rope was ready and became tight. He signaled to us that it was time to go. Ever so slightly, I increased power, and then we lost sight of him. He may have risen out of the water a foot or so, then disappeared, and snap! The rope was jerked out of his hands, and so we circled back. We gave it another try and again, the same result. It was as if we were dragging a thousand-pound log out of the water. It just was not happening. I don't remember who came up with it, but someone on the boat suggested that we needed to sort of jerk him up out of the water. If you start too slowly, the force of the water becomes too great and works against you. So, armed with that bit of info, we circled back for yet another try. I gunned it. Snap! This time the only thing coming out of the water, other than Uncle Wesley's teeth, was the ski rope, which we all immediately had to hit the deck to keep from being decapitated with. When I think about it, he really is lucky he kept his arms in tact after that trip.

So, again, we circled back. This time, we got the speed right and up he came. Although, not for long. Almost immediately, he took a face plant into the choppy water that clapped with an alarming intensity. We circled back again. After reassuring us he was still alive, he went for it again. Again, an unbelievable wipeout. When he surfaced, I watched him slap his hand on the water's surface in disgust. We circled back again. Then his son, Joshua, wanted to give it a try. So, the young buck gave it a try and produced the same result time and time again. Even the strength of youth wasn't going to cut it. But Uncle Wesley was determined he was going to teach us how to master the wakeboard. However, up and then down was all we achieved. Again and again, we circled back. It was so bad that everyone on the boat became nauseous from all the circles we completed. However, each time, the intensity on Uncle Wesley's face grew more stern than the last.

Finally, he was up and everyone was shouting. We went twenty yards or so, and then all of a sudden, he disappeared headfirst over the wakeboard. When he surfaced, the scene was ugly. He had a pop-knot on his forehead and his lip was bleeding. So, of course we beg him to stop and do something else. I'm not sure we wanted to stop for his benefit or it was the fact that we were too sick to ride anymore. Either way, we all wanted it to stop. Then something happened that I will never forget. Uncle Wesley lifts his hand into the air and points straight up with the number one sign, and says, "Just one more time." "Are you serious?" I said! Again, he signals the number one and says, "Just one more time."

At this point, you want me to tell you that we conquered the wakeboard that day. Well, we did not. And we did not for some time after that day. It was a long and arduous process. But that day formed our motto: "Just one more time." By the end of the day, his lip was bleeding, his forehead was red, and he just surfaced from one more nasty fall and he said again, "Just one more time." Crazy? Sure it was, but what an experience. Tired, hurting, and the body was aching, but I've got to try one more time.

That is the whole point to this chapter. You, yes, you! You have got to try just one more time. I know you're hurt. You're spiritually bleeding and every part of you screams that you have just got to stop this madness and never come back. But wait! I've got a simple question for you. Where is it written or what law was passed that states when you fail that you're finished and you're through? Where did we pick that up? It sure wasn't grade school or high school or even college, I'm sure. Remember, if at first you first don't succeed, try, try again. Seems odd to you now that you are older, doesn't? But as a kid, it gave you license to dream. No matter how many times you did not get it right, you went for it anyway. The more you were told that you could not do it, the more you tried. What happened to us? Where did we lose our drive?

There is a phenomenon that has crept into the spiritual (church) world that has puzzled me. When someone fails, there seems to be that law that applies that says, well, you've blown it and it's over for you. You will never be anything again.

My friend, you have just got to try one more time. Proverbs 24:16 says, *the godly may trip seven times, but they will get up again. But one disaster is enough to overthrow the wicked.* Could it be that your refusal to get up just one more time is really the sin that God holds against you? Not getting up again is really the sign of your wickedness to the world. Not getting back up is saying that God is not big enough and what he did for us at Calvary was not good enough for you. What if Thomas Edison stopped after failing as much as he did? If I have the story right, he tried 1000 times to invent different things, but failed every time until the 1001st time. At that moment, he invented the light bulb. And the truth of the matter is that he failed the 1001st time as well, but invented the light bulb by accident.

We live in the fast food/microwave era that says I have got to have it now and I have got to have it my way. Just as that kind of food will shorten your lifespan, it will also shorten the lifespan of your ministry. You have got to try just one more time again, again, and again. Then one day you will get it. You will glide across the waters of your life's ministry. Let me say this: a great deal of your success in wakeboarding is determined by what waters you choose to ride. Too choppy, and you're going to buy it every time. Choose your water well, but for goodness sake, get out there on the water!

Now let me say a few things about those who are driving the boat. If you remember, our struggle in getting my uncle out of the water was that we were too slow in the beginning. Then we throttled too high and nearly jerked his arms out of socket. But after awhile, we got the speed right. Most likely, you know someone right now who is struggling to get up on the water again due to a traumatic failure in his/her life. They're not dead, they're just sitting in the water, hoping they can tread it long enough to survive, and maybe everyone that knew their situation will somehow forget it and allow them back into the boat. But back in the boat is not where they belong. That's not their calling yet. So, you now have the opportunity to get them back on their feet. If you move too slowly, you will never get them out. The weight of their situation will be just too much to overcome. But if you try and put them right back on the surface too quickly, they will not be able to handle it and will ultimately fall again.

In the church world, there are few who really know how to deal with those who fail. They just cannot seem to get the speed right.

So, we tell them well, you may not be able to get out on the open water again, but I will put you in the boat. Again, that is not where they belong. They belong out there. You know the place, where Jesus walks on the water. Why do you suppose that Peter is the only one that walked on the water, excluding the fact that he was the only one that asked the Lord to bid him? I believe it was because Peter was destined to be out there on the water. The first time, Peter was young and growing and had just enough faith to give it a try. The second time, when he saw Jesus after the crucifixion, Peter once again was out there on the water, swimming. Now understand something. He was just coming off the heels of a major failure. I don't care what anyone thinks, denying Christ is a pretty major problem. In today's standards, that is pretty close to blasphemy. Not once, not twice, but three times Peter made his desire known that night. He did not want anything to do with Jesus. But when we see Jesus walking on the seashore, he did not wait like the rest of the crew. He went back on the water. So why was Peter chosen, if you will, to walk on the water that night? Because Jesus wanted the Peters of our world to know that there is no better time to get back out there on the water than just after a fall. So for those of you who are driving the boat, you have got to try and get them back up just one more time. That's why you are driving. That's your calling.

I cannot give you the correct speed for every situation. You have to feel that out yourself. But you have definitely got to get them back up. Jesus did. That fact is that they are going to fall over and over again. They will get up and fall because they will concentrate too much on the waves and the things around them. James 1:2 says to *count it all joy when you fall into diverse temptations (trials)*. Notice it says *when*. That fact is that everyone in the boat is going to get dizzy, and I mean sick to his stomach, trying to get those who have fallen back on the water. It is a trial of your faith and it will push you to the limit. But when you get them back up, you will never regret it. The sickness subsides and stability returns to your organization. When it's all said and done, you will notice that your own ministry will take on a different feel. It should. You should feel more like him.

Final Thoughts

Chapter 21

The Prescription for
Restoration Identified

If you are honest with yourself, throughout this entire book you have been waiting for me to give you an exact Biblical (or otherwise) prescription for restoring leaders. I pray that you are not like some that skip to the back of the book and try to finish it without reading the previous chapters. It is vitally important that you read this book thoroughly and considered each and every scriptural reference, example, story, and suggestion. If you are a follower of Christ then he is, without debate, the best and most perfect example of how to handle fallen leaders. He did a great job with Peter, by the way.

I have heard the statement made once, "Yeah, but that was before Peter received the baptism of the Holy Spirit and was baptized in Jesus' name." I almost laughed out loud when I heard that. I smiled back at him and then responded with this question: "When were the disciples considered the disciples?" He just looked at me with this blank look like I just committed some kind of heresy. I asked the question again. Then he responded with less enthusiasm than a koala bear on a hot summer's day, "Well, before Pentecost." This, he quietly uttered as if someone would report him to the Sanhedrin. Peter was a follower of Christ long before his Pentecostal experience and subsequent message to the masses. Let me say this: we need to be careful not to unfairly judge someone's journey to Christ. There is always more for people to reach for, regardless of where they are in their walk toward Christ.

This leads me to my discovery of the prescription for restoration. I almost fell out of my chair when I saw it. There it was, right in front of me the whole time, and I just overlooked it a thousand times. I just could not believe how simple it was. There is no way this could be for real. I mean, the complexities of restoration are such that anything so simple would just not be adequate. I hope you are ready for this, because this is huge and will radically change your ideals forever. Here it is.

1 Corinthians 13

> [1] If I could speak all the languages of earth and of angels, but didn't love others, I would only be a noisy gong or a clanging cymbal. [2] If I had the gift of prophecy, and if I understood all of God's secret plans and possessed all knowledge, and if I had such faith that I could move mountains, but didn't love others, I would be nothing. [3] If I gave everything I have to the poor and even sacrificed my body, I could boast about it; but if I didn't love others, I would have gained nothing.

> [4] Love is patient and kind. Love is not jealous or boastful or proud [5] or rude. It does not demand its own way. It is not irritable, *and it keeps no record of being wronged* (emphasis mine). [6] It does not rejoice about injustice but rejoices whenever the truth wins out. [7] Love never gives up, never loses faith, is always hopeful, and endures through every circumstance.

[8] Prophecy and speaking in unknown languages and special knowledge will become useless. But love will last forever! [9] Now our knowledge is partial and incomplete, and even the gift of prophecy reveals only part of the whole picture! [10] But when full understanding comes, these partial things will become useless.

[11] When I was a child, I spoke and thought and reasoned as a child. But when I grew up, I put away childish things. [12] Now we see things imperfectly as in a cloudy mirror, but then we will see everything with perfect clarity. All that I know now is partial and incomplete, but then I will know everything completely, just as God now knows me completely.

[13] Three things will last forever—faith, hope, and love—and the greatest of these is love.

Here it is, after all the hours of study, research, and writing. This one chapter completely arrests me. We all know it as the chapter of love. It has been quoted more times in my ears than almost any other Scripture, yet I completely forgot about it. Maybe that's why love is called the greatest. If we ever truly get it, there is nothing that we can't do or succeed in. Just a thought.

The subject of restoration is a very stressful and difficult one to handle. Every time a church is faced with this issue, everyone is looking for that magic button to make it all go away or fix instantly. Sorry, no easy button here. I have a sneaking suspicion that if we applied 1 Corinthians 13 to every case of failure that happens to our leaders, we could quite possibly change our world. How many people would look at the church in a different light if they saw how we handled the failures of leaders? How much more would they trust the church with their failures? I think it would astound us. Our buildings would not hold the droves of people that would come.

If you will notice, I highlighted for you the part in verse 5 that says "keeps no record of being wronged." I guess it really all comes down to forgiveness. If we have true love, then we will restore those that have fallen and love them unconditionally. I witnessed one man to say, "We love them and they can come to church anytime they want. They just can't ever hold a position or ordination with this church again." I am sorry. That just flies in the face of Scripture and is not Christlike.

I want to continue to address the mindset just mentioned from a different angle. Recently, I posed a question on my Facebook page, asking if, when leaders fall, should they or can they be restored. The question raised a lively debate, of which I was ever grateful for. The issue that was raised was what sins we can be restored from and what sins we can't be restored from. My personal belief is that we can be restored from any sin. After speaking with Pastor Wesley McClain on the issue, he brought up a great and wonderful point. He stated, "One side of the debate feels there should be limits on restoration or what can be restored. The other side feels that we cannot place limits on what can be restored in any manner. Both are correct and both are wrong." This was a great entry of thought and one that I felt needed to be pursued further. He continued that, "The very fact is, sin always has a price regardless that the blood of Christ cleanses us from our sins. That price can come in many forms. You murder someone, you will go to prison. You steal money from the church, you will not be trusted for some time and maybe not ever." As we continued our discussion, we came to this understanding. There are limits placed on everyone who sins; it's by default. No matter what the sin, there will be limits placed on you by the very act of what you committed. So the attempt to place limits on people is useless because their sins accomplish that automatically. To try and release someone from those limits is useless because leadership is about leading people, and if no one trusts the now debunked leader, then that attempt is futile at best. *Sin places limits on all who succumb to it.* There is no way around it and there is no way of improving on it. There are certain laws of nature that happen without assistance every day. Nothing you or I can do will change it, help it, or rearrange it. In fact, I think we all have seen the calamity of trying to mess with these laws when Hurricane Katrina came to town. I'm sorry; it's just not a smart thing to build a city below sea level within a hundred feet of the sea. The same goes with the issue of restoration. We mess things up so badly when we try and alter the effects either way.

So what do we do then, you may ask? We stop trying to mess with the process from both sides. The conservative side need not try and legislate restoration and the moderate side of the issue needs to stop trying to remove the God-given laws and effects of sin. We are only responsible for biblically restoring these fallen leaders as the Scripture states. (Referenced in chapter two of this book, if you forgot.) Time, place, and the person, along with the hand of God, will determine to what, when, or where the fallen leader will be restored. It is not for the onlookers to involve themselves with.

The final point is this. Love has to be the main ingredient in every situation of leadership failure and membership failure. We can't approach it from hierarchies of wisdom and experience; it must be approached in love. Let love guide you in every case. We get so used to allowing our procedures and manuals to show us how to handle the fallen. How many of those manuals were written with 1 Corinthians 13 in mind? Our manuals and procedures become doctrine to us at times, and that is failure all of its own. 1 Corinthians 13 states emphatically that our education, our gifts of the Spirit, our faith, our generosity, and self-sacrifice will all come to end. They are all temporal and only vehicles to get us from point A to point B. That's it. They will not save us or keep us forever. However, the only constant there will be is that of *love*.

Jesus is hanging on a cross with blood running down his face and experiencing pain unimaginable to us today. He looks down to the earth below to the very ones that have caused him this agony. With sweat and blood filling his mouth, he utters the most loving statement anyone could ever speak. "Father forgive them for they know not what they do." And we can't fully restore and love our brother or sister because they have failed? Jesus never uttered what they did to him. He never spoke out what their sin was or exposed the failures in their lives. He simply looked at them with love and did the only thing love could do. He died for them while reconciling and restoring a world full of failures.

Chapter 22

Now it's Your Turn

In the proceeding chapters, I have shared with you my story and the story of nine other leaders who succumbed to their human weaknesses. I also shared with you the stories of some of the most popular figures in the Bible and how they failed, and yet they are the subject of some of the greatest sermons we have ever preached or listened to. We have explored numerous scriptural accounts of Christ's ministry in restoration.

As I stated in the introduction, it was never my intent for this book to be the authority on the matter of restoration. However, I do have a unique viewpoint and experience that most do not. Be that as it may, I only desire to start a worldwide discussion within all denominations and organizations concerning failed leaders. Failed leaders have existed from the beginning of time and they will continue to show up until the end of time. We can no longer ignore this fact and place them on the shelves of "once was." We must find a way to restore our fallen leaders. More importantly, we must find a way to create more accountability to head off the failures of our precious leaders before they get to this point. We must find a solution to give assurance to our leaders that they have a place to go when they find themselves tempted, weak, and hurting.

There are leaders out there right now that are in the throes of temptation, weakness, and utter despair and we don't even know it. The problem is not the temptation or what they are experiencing. It is the fact that they have no place to run to for fear of ridicule, judgment, and rejection. They need a place to turn, just like the people they pastor and lead. With this book, I am calling for every organization and every religious society to establish such a place, a secret place.

James 5:16 tells us to confess our faults one to another that we may be healed. If you look at the original writings, this can be quoted like the following. *Confess one to another your issues, so you will have the power to heal and be healed.* James was trying to tell the church that within its halls, we have the power to heal. I am not talking about the power of Christ's stripes or the power of his name concerning healing of our bodies. I am talking about the power to heal us of our weaknesses as humans. When we have someone we can confess to and they in turn can confess to us, it actually heals us of our temptations. It also gives us the power to heal others. When I allow others to confess to me, it will bring to the forefront my own weaknesses and cause me to expose my own self to them, thus bringing total and complete accountability and a level playing field.

Now it's your turn. It is your turn to find someone and start confessing. Now it's your turn for someone to find you and confess to you without fear of retribution and condemnation. Do you have the power to heal? If you confess your faults, you will. But if you hold back because you, too, fear the outcome, you will continue to live with your illness and lack power to heal and be healed.

Now it's time for every organization, every pastor, and every leader to start healing our fallen leaders. It won't be too hard to find them. You may only need to look as close as the next mirror.

Notes

Chapter 2

E-Sword, Galatians 6:1, King James Version
E-Sword, Romans 3:23, King James Version
E-Sword, 1 John 1:8, King James Version
E-Sword, James 4:17, King James Version

4152 Pneumatikos a, GK: 4461 [- 4154], spiritual, pertaining to the Spirit; (n.) Spiritual person. (Strong's Concordance 2001 by Zondervan)

2675 v. GK: restore kataartizo. to restore, put in order, mend; to make complete, equip, train; to prepare, ordain:-perfect, make perfect, mending, fitted, framed, perfected, perfectly joined together, prepared, restore. (Strong's Concordance 2001 by Zondervan)

Chapter 3

E-Sword, Book of Jonah, King James Version

Chapter 4

Luke 15, King James Version
E-Sword, Isaiah 64:6, King James Version
E-Sword, Romans 10:14
E-Sword, Isaiah 53:6
Barna Group survey as found in *Unchristian* by Baker Books.
Authors David Kennaman and Gabe Lyons

Chapter 5

John 11, King James Version
E-Sword, Romans 11:29, King James Version
James 1, King James Version

Chapter 6

E-Sword, Matthew 19:4, American Standard Version
E-Sword, Matthew 19:8, American Standard Version
E-Sword, Malachi 3:6, King James Version
E-Sword, Luke 9:26, King James Version
E-Sword, Romans 11:29, King James Version

Chapter 7

Thanks to Pastor Clint Brown as he ministered this topic to me
E-Sword, Luke 15:4, King James Version
E-Sword, Jeremiah 29:11, King James Version
E-Sword, Isaiah 9:6, King James Version
E-Sword, Amos 3:11-12, King James Version

Chapter 8

Quote from *Knights Master Book of 4,000 Illustrations* by Walter
B. Knight Copyright 1956 Wm. B. Eerdmans Publishing Co.

Chapter 9

BibleGateway.com, Matthew 1:1-16, King James Version

Chapter 10

E-Sword, *Matthew Henry's Commentary*
E-Sword, *Barnes' Notes*
E-Sword, 1 Timothy 5, King James Version

Chapter 11

The Wizard of Oz (1939) is a copyrighted name and used in reference only.

Chapter 12

Personal story of John used by permission.

Chapter 13

Your God Is Too Safe by Mark Buchannan copyright 2001 Multnomah Publishing.
E-Sword, Romans 8:28, New Living Translation
Zechariah 12:6, King James Version

Chapter 14

Talent is Never Enough by John Maxwell copyright 2007 Published by Thomas Nelson, Inc.
E-Sword, Proverbs 4:23, King James Version
Quote by Henry Perry Liddon as written in *Talent is Never Enough* by John Maxwell copyright 2007 Published by Thomas Nelson, Inc.

Quote by George Washington as written in *Talent is Never Enough* by John Maxwell copyright 2007 Published by Thomas Nelson, Inc.

Chapter 15

Webster's Dictionary 1950s College Edition
E-Sword, 1 Kings 3:9, King James Version

OT:8085 shama` (shaw-mah'); a primitive root; to hear intelligently (often with implication of attention, obedience, etc.; causatively, to tell, etc.): .(Strong's Concordance 2001 by Zondervan)

E-Sword, Proverbs 16:1, King James Version

"Aim High," "Be All that you can Be," "We're Looking for a Few Good Men." All slogans referenced are the property of their corresponding branches of military services of the United States Government.

E-Sword, 1 Samuel 9:2, King James Version
E-Sword, 1 Samuel 15:22, King James Version
E-Sword, Romans 12:3, King James Version
E-Sword, 1 Chronicles 22:12, King James Version
E-Sword, Matthew 8:9, King James Version
E-Sword, Acts 13:22, King James Version
E-Sword, Philippians 2:88, King James Version
E-Sword, Matthew 16:26 New Living Translation

Chapter 18

E-Sword, Psalms 91:11, King James Version
E-Sword, Psalms 27:5, King James Version
E-Sword, Psalms 31:20, King James Version
E-Sword, Psalms 32:7, King James Version

Chapter 19

Quote from *Knight's Master Book of 4,000 Illustrations* by Walter B. Knight Copyright 1956 Wm. B. Eerdmans Publishing Co.

Chapter 20

E-Sword, Proverbs 24:6, New Living Translation
E-Sword, James 1:2, King James Version

Chapter 21

BibleGateway.com, 1 Corinthians 13, New Living Translation

Chapter 22

E-Sword, James 5:16, King James Version